The Dr. Li's Diet Cookbook

365 Days of Easy-to-Follow Recipes Inspired by Dr. William W Li's Teachings for a Longer and Healthier Life

Rebecca Griffin

© 2025 by Rebecca Griffin

All rights reserved. No part of this book may be copied, reproduced, stored, or transmitted in any form or by any means without the prior written permission of the author, except for brief quotations used in reviews or articles.

Disclaimer

This book is inspired by the teachings of Dr. William W. Li but is independently written and published by Rebecca Griffin. The content is for informational and educational purposes only and does not constitute medical advice. Please consult a qualified healthcare provider before making any changes to your diet or health routine.

About The Author

Dr. William W. Li, MD, is a globally recognized physician, scientist, author, and speaker renowned for his pioneering work in medical research and public health. As the President, Medical Director, and co-founder of the Angiogenesis Foundation, Dr. Li has significantly influenced the development of treatments for over 70 diseases, including cancer, diabetes, blindness, heart disease, and obesity.

Dr. Li earned his A.B. with honors in Biochemistry from Harvard College and obtained his M.D. from the University of Pittsburgh School of Medicine. He completed his residency and clinical fellowship in General Internal Medicine at Massachusetts General Hospital, a Harvard teaching hospital.

Under Dr. Li's leadership, the Angiogenesis Foundation has played a central role in bringing about modern treatments for various conditions, including nine different cancers, chronic wounds, and skin diseases. His work has led to the development of 34 FDA-approved treatments for cancer, blindness, and wound healing, impacting over 50 million people worldwide.

Dr. Li's research has been published in leading scientific journals such as Science, The New England Journal of Medicine, The Lancet, and Nature Reviews. He has held faculty appointments at Harvard Medical School, Tufts University, and Dartmouth Medical School.

A significant focus of Dr. Li's work is on the concept of "food as medicine." He advocates for using nutrition-based approaches to activate the body's health defense systems to prevent and reduce human suffering. His TED Talk, "Can We Eat to Starve Cancer?", has garnered over 11 million views, highlighting the impact of diet on health.

Dr. Li is the author of the New York Times bestseller Eat to Beat Disease: The New Science of How Your Body Can Heal Itself, where he presents the science behind over 200 foods that help the body heal. His work emphasizes the importance of diet in disease prevention and health promotion.

Preface

When I first encountered Dr. William W. Li's work, I was struck by a simple yet revolutionary idea: what we eat has the power to heal. His research—fueled by decades of clinical science, groundbreaking discoveries in disease treatment, and a passion for preventive health—offered something both profound and practical: a blueprint for using food as medicine to extend not just our lifespan, but our healthspan.

As a globally recognized physician, scientist, and author, Dr. Li's legacy in advancing medical breakthroughs is extraordinary. He has helped pioneer treatments for over 70 diseases and been at the forefront of research connecting diet to cellular health, immunity, metabolism, and even the ability to starve cancer. But what makes his message resonate on a deeply human level is its accessibility—anyone, regardless of background, budget, or cooking skill, can harness the power of healing through the foods they choose each day.

This cookbook was born out of that very promise.

Over the years, I've worked with individuals navigating a wide range of health challenges—cancer survivors rebuilding their strength, individuals with chronic inflammation seeking relief, parents looking to nourish their children better, and even people who simply wanted more energy and clarity throughout their day. Across every story, the common denominator was this: food mattered. But it wasn't just about what to eat; it was about how to cook it, how to enjoy it, and how to make it a sustainable part of daily life.

That's where this book comes in.

The Purpose Behind the Pages

This cookbook is more than a collection of recipes—it's a daily companion for anyone looking to thrive. Each of the recipes is inspired by the teachings of Dr. Li and designed to be more than just healthy. They are functional, aiming to activate the body's five health defense systems: angiogenesis (the growth of healthy blood vessels), regeneration (via stem cells), microbiome support, DNA protection, and immunity boosting. Whether you're blending a smoothie, preparing a hearty soup, or roasting a dinner that brings your whole family to the table, you're not just cooking—you're participating in your own health story.

You'll also find that these recipes do not sacrifice taste for function. Food, after all, should bring joy. Using ingredients like wild blueberries, turmeric, extra virgin olive oil, mushrooms, dark chocolate, and green tea, each recipe is crafted to deliver maximum flavor and maximum benefit. I truly believe that the healthiest foods on Earth are also the most delicious—when prepared with care, tradition, and a bit of creativity.

A Personal Journey Rooted in Science and Soul

My journey as a culinary wellness advocate has been shaped by science, culture, and countless conversations with elders, doctors, patients, and everyday people from around the world. From my early days learning to cook beside my mother, to cooking alongside longevity experts in places like Okinawa and Greece, I've come to understand the power of food from both ancestral wisdom and modern research.

This duality is embedded in the recipes you'll discover here. You'll see nods to traditional healing techniques—like using garlic to support immunity or drinking bone broth to nourish the gut—alongside cutting-edge insights into how certain compounds in food can influence gene expression or support mitochondrial health. This blend of old and new is not just beautiful; it's essential. It's how we make lasting changes.

How to Use This Book

You don't need to be a chef to get started. Whether you're a beginner looking for a step-by-step guide or an experienced home cook eager for fresh inspiration, this book is organized to support your goals. Each recipe is clear, accessible, and labeled with its nutritional highlights. There's something here for every season, every dietary need, and every craving—from energizing breakfasts to comforting soups, vibrant salads, satisfying mains, and guilt-free desserts.

Additionally, you'll find practical advice woven throughout—from how to stock a longevity-based pantry to tips on food storage, batch cooking, and using herbs and spices for both flavor and function.

Think of this book as a toolbox, a playbook, and a cheerleader all in one.

Looking Ahead

As you turn these pages, I invite you to see food not as a restriction, but as an opportunity. An opportunity to take control of your health. An opportunity to experience joy, flavor, and connection. An opportunity to nourish not only your body but your entire being.

Dr. Li's work has shown us that the path to better health doesn't begin in a hospital or a pharmacy. It begins in the kitchen.

And now, it begins with you.

Introduction

I've been promoting healthy eating habits for over a decade.

My key tool has been flavour, as I demonstrated how exceptional taste and nutrition can coexist peacefully at the dinner table. Flavour is an excellent, and often necessary, agent of dietary adjustment. I have a buddy who says, "If something doesn't taste good, people won't eat it in the long run, no matter how good it is for them." I always knew science would be a powerful motivator for my healing journey.

That day has arrived. As with any burgeoning field, the study of nutrition, particularly diet in relation to longevity, has taken several decades to gain traction. The fact that I can now write on the links between diet and longevity based on thousands of published scientific studies rather than speculation fills me with confidence to the point of bursting. It's as if scientists all over the world have validated what Grandma already knew when she said, "Eat this. It is excellent for you."

It's evident to me that, as a society, we're embracing—or at least very interested in—living not just long lives, but long healthy lives, and doing so at least in part through the foods we consume. Just look at the New York Times best-seller list in recent years; multiple chart-topping books have dug into the subject, with writers travelling the world to figure out why individuals in particular locations live much longer lives. In several cases, diet appeared to have an important influence. Research has explored the relationship between diet and the body, as well as other aspects such as exercise, community involvement, purpose, and relaxation strategies to manage stress.

As a chef with a master's degree in nutrition, I've always been fascinated by that synergy.

I'll be honest: flavour (and some lovely scents) drew me to the kitchen in the first place. I've been a cook since I was six years old, sitting on the kitchen counter with my mother and helping her create anything from brownies to soup. Even then, I had an instinctual knowledge of which foods were nourishing and which were more of an indulgence than beneficial to me. And, unlike other children, I usually discovered that the most flavourful foods triggered my "yes!" response. I never had to be convinced to eat ripe wild Maine blueberries or broccoli, which I believed looked like trees. All these years later, it's tremendously exciting to hear experts reveal that eating blueberries can also improve memory and broccoli can help prevent cancer. If you're going to twist my arm...

The reality is, I believe we are all born with an instinct that directs us towards the meals that nourish us the most. That instinct most likely originated as a survival trait, but many individuals today have lost touch with this inner intelligence.

The Art of Yum!

Rest assured that the content in this book is not based on my kitchen countertop wisdom. I spoke with a number of renowned physicians, nutritionists, and academics who have conducted extensive research on nutrition and lifespan. Their expertise informs every recipe—and nearly every word—in this book. After all, we can't completely grasp how foods affect our health and wellness unless we use good science, which means conducting rigorous, peer-reviewed research.

If that seems a little dry, here's some good news: the most healthy foods are ones that most of us already know and enjoy. (And if you don't already love some of them, I bet you will after trying the recipes in this book.) Consider the Super Sixteen—foods that contain the highest levels of antioxidants, which help eliminate free radicals from the body. These ancient foods also include high levels of healthful omega-3 fats, probiotics, and other phytochemicals, vitamins, and minerals that benefit the body.

Perhaps not surprisingly, the Super Sixteen contain a variety of other health-promoting minerals. So, what is the Super Sixteen?

Here they are, alphabetical order:

- Asparagus
- Avocado
- Basil (and mint, which is in the same family)
- Blueberries (and other dark berries)
- Coffee
- Dark chocolate
- Garlic
- Green tea
- Kale
- Olive oil
- Pomegranates
- Sweet potatoes
- Thyme
- Walnuts
- Wild salmon
- Yogurt

Isn't this surprising? Contrary to popular

belief, eating the most nutritious foods is not a chore; rather, it will satisfy your palette. Take a look at the list again. What are you seeing? Veggies, fruits, seafood, nuts, herbs, and chocolate. Yes, you read that right: chocolate.

And that's only the top 16. Every ingredient in this book is packed with nutrients and taste. As you browse through this book, you'll notice that many are already family and personal favorites. And if you've fallen out of the habit of cooking, familiarity can serve as a motivator to get you back in the kitchen.

The Wisdom of Our Elders

In a nutshell, I meet smart, motivated people every day—people like you, dear reader—who want to get serious about eating healthy. They want to figure out how to apply the abundance of nutritional research to create wonderful meals, but they don't know where to begin. Fortunately, I believe I can provide a culinary clue. Instead of seeking futuristic solutions like meal-in-a-pills or food replicators, I propose addressing our current culinary challenges in the past. We need to consult our seniors, the nanas, who have a lifetime of culinary experience.

It's fantastic that science has advanced to the point where it can tell us 10 reasons why ginger is excellent for the digestive tract. But, Grandma? Perhaps she never earned an advanced degree (not many did in the old country), but she was aware that when children drank ginger tea, they stopped complaining about their stomachaches.

As you read and utilize this book, you will notice that I have searched out and provided traditional wisdom to supplement the science and flavor laboratory results with real-world information. After all, science can't be the one to wag the dog. I'm not sure about you, but I have never seen a list of phytochemicals that made me salivate.

To help you love cooking and get the most out of this book, I met with elders from well-known longevity hotspots such as Okinawa, Greece, and Sweden, who have passed down years of cooking wisdom. They learned to cook from their grandmothers, who were typically women who regarded food as a way to connect families to the soil and promote wellness. This perspective may be more common among those who rely on gardens and farms for their food.

The skill to nurture, which can be learned and shared, is extremely powerful. Dorothy, the woman I spoke with, informed me about her 102-year-old grandmother's reputation as a culinary healer. Every day came another tap on the door or word of an injury or illness that needed attention. Her grandma would listen, nod sagely, and then toddle off to the kitchen. The house would soon be filled with soothing aromas, such as homemade applesauce, strawberry and rhubarb compote, or hot tea made from cornhusks with ginger and honey. Young Dorothy would receive a container with a bow and instructions. Her grandma would remark, "Take this to Miss Constance across the street and tell her I'll be right over," before gently turning the child's shoulder toward the door with a worn hand.

We all have memories of seeing food in that healing light that we may call on when needed. For Dorothy, eating healthily became especially vital in times of stress —something she knew plenty about because of her position as a police chief. Long hours, bad coffee, and terrible eating habits came with the territory. She couldn't do much about the first two, but she wouldn't tolerate terrible meals for herself or her crew. Every time a difficult case had her investigators in knots, she brought in homecooked meals. That's what I consider a morale booster! After retiring, she continued her grandmother's legacy by preparing meals for the chronically ill and sharing her "joy tea" with visitors.

Several grandmothers have helped me feel a similar connection and reconnection with the healing power of food. I emphasize reconnection because, like many Americans, I used to eat on the go and engage in other unhealthy eating patterns when I was younger. My return to the kitchen was an unplanned side effect of staying with Signoria Rizzo, an Italian grandmother who welcomed visitors from other countries. I guess I was more (or less) than she bargained for. She didn't speak English, and I only spoke a few words of Italian, but when she saw me in the kitchen, the message in her pitying eyes was clear: this one can't even cook spaghetti.

But rather than dismissing me as hopeless, she accepted me as her science project. I became an Eliza Doolittle of sorts, but instead of singing or balancing books on my head, I had to learn how to cook. After all, from Signora Rizzo's old-world perspective, it was necessary if I was to find a husband. Of course, learning to cook successfully also required learning to shop, which in Italy entails daily trips to the market. I joined a group consisting of Signora Rizzo, a dozen white-haired friends, and myself. Harpo Marx would have been pleased: using just pantomime, Signora Rizzo demonstrated how to feel up (there's simply no other term for it) every piece of produce in the market. In her opinion, this was not a luxury, but rather an economic necessity. Who had the money to waste on rotten produce? Signora Rizzo's acquaintances initially mocked me as a newcomer. But over time—and a lot of meals—I gained their trust and discovered mine.

I'm telling you all this for a reason. Learning to eat for life and prepare healthy (and delicious) meals is a gradual process that benefits from positive reinforcement. It occurs on virtually a subconscious level. It can be especially beneficial to start with foods you already appreciate, such as the Super Sixteen. It's easier to include a new ingredient, such as a herb or spice, when it's coupled with a cuisine you already enjoy. I know that when the basis is known, I'm more likely to take a risk and try something new.

As you become more attentive of your food choices, you will become more aware of the relationship between what you eat and how you feel. This is what happened to me in Italy. The healthy, life-enhancing eating habits I'd been introduced to were expansive and exhilarating. It was a gift from the nonnas, and all they asked in return was that I share it with others.

Okay, they didn't ask that directly, but their lifestyle said volumes. They lived to pass on their culinary expertise, including their wisdom on the connections between food and lifespan.

It was undoubtedly their most valuable possession, and passing the torch marked an entry into the responsibility of caring not only for oneself, but also for one's family and community.

I took their message and tactics to heart. When I got home, I began cooking for others, most of whom were coping with chronic illnesses. Many of them had cancer and were naturally afraid to eat because of the negative effects of the treatment. Some individuals with lifestyle-related disorders, including diabetes, heart disease, and autoimmune diseases, although being on restricted diets, still sought specific flavors. I began operating in a role I subsequently coined "culinary translator"—determining people's requirements and then providing them with wholesome, tasty whole food meals that left them satisfied.

Over the last decade, via thousands of hours of conversation with colleagues and clients, I've perfected my knowledge and streamlined the process of preparing healthy meals. With the growing interest in eating for life, I decided to develop a book that translates my experience, scientific findings, and ancient wisdom into tasty, wholesome meals for everyone to enjoy. As you read and use this book, I hope you feel as if you have a kind, helpful presence in your kitchen, offering ideas, support, and advice—perhaps a grandmother whose greatest wish for you is a long, healthy, and happy life.

Chapter 1
Food, Nutrition, and Your Body

I want to take you on an unbelievable adventure that encompasses every cell in your body and every fiber of that most magical creature: yourself.

When I first began cooking seriously, many of my fellow cooks and other colleagues in the field of wellness believed that great-tasting food bursting with nutrients could also act as medicine —a belief we held based on our own upbringing and the way so many cultures use food for healing. Even if it wasn't that long ago, we didn't have much scientific evidence to back up our beliefs.

Now we do. Since the 1980s, the number of nutritional research published in peer-reviewed scientific publications has doubled every decade. Overall, serious researchers at leading academic medical institutes in the United States and around the world have published almost 250,000 nutritional studies, including over 100,000 since the turn of the millennium. From my stove-front perspective, this means that I can point to practically any item and know that someone with a long list of qualifications has researched how that food affects health and specific body systems, from head to toe, inside and out.

This information empowers us to choose enjoyable and nutritious foods, giving us more control over our health and longevity. Do these foods need to be delicious? You bet. Because, as said in the opening, no matter how nutritious a food is, if it isn't tasty, you won't eat it on a regular basis.

I know that people enjoy playing with favorable odds. And I understand that you're probably thinking if eating healthy will ensure that you live to be a centenarian. Maybe. Maybe not. What you eat can improve your quality of life and extend your life, regardless of your health status, according to study.

If you're already healthy, consuming the correct meals will help maintain your cellular energy and immune system intact, preventing the natural deterioration of these systems as you age. And if you're well but your family history of illness has your forehead furrowed like a shar-pei's, here's a shocking reality that should function as mental Botox: your genes aren't always your destiny. Eating certain meals can impact genetic expression, which decides which DNA sequences are converted into bodily chemicals. Simply said, gene expression directs your cells' actions, such as protein synthesis, and when they should occur. Certain meals may suppress the same cellular triggers that, when activated, have caused specific diseases in your parents, grandparents, and other family members.

Nutrition can be beneficial for those who are seriously unwell. The correct meals can accomplish wonders, from jumpstarting the process of making healthy cells to replacing those that have been damaged or diseased, to lowering pharmaceutical side effects and enhancing the body's ability to detoxify drugs after they have completed their function.

I frequently lead workshops where people learn how to reconnect with nutritious cuisine. I enjoy showing students how specific foods can nourish their cells, organs, tissues, and other physiological systems, resulting in a sense of well-being. That is exactly what I intend to do in the following chapter: demonstrate many of the delightful linkages between exceptional flavors, power-packed nutrition, and longevity. This section serves as a beginning point for a culinary experience, connecting recipes, delectable foods, helpful nutrients, and their effects on health and life.

Where should I start? To understand how meals affect the body, you must first understand how the body functions, specifically how it metabolizes food. So let's start with some fundamental knowledge about the body's processes.

The Beginning

When you first started out in life, you were nothing more than a single cell whose sole purpose was to reproduce. Congratulate yourself on a job well done, because you now consist of 100 trillion cells that sustain ten major organ systems.

Discuss managerial difficulties! The body requires a wide range of nutrients to function, including macronutrients (carbs, proteins, and fats), vitamins, minerals, and a long list of phytochemicals (beneficial compounds found in fruits and vegetables), ranging from anthocyanidins to zeaxanthin. However, for a hundred thousand years, humans survived on whatever they could scavenge, and their bodies did an excellent job of adjusting to whatever fuel was available.

We've come a long way since our hunter-gatherer days, and in recent decades, the science of nutrition has grown almost as rapidly as the cells in your body have since conception. In fact, that is where we should begin: with a brief introduction of the science—specifically, the science of the processes that lead from your first day as a single cell to the magnificent complexity that you are now reading this book: epigenetics.

Epigenetics

The truth is that, of all the nutrition studies that have been conducted, few have looked into whether a single food or vitamin may help you live longer. The explanation is straightforward: reality is complex. Numerous factors influence human longevity, ranging from our genes (about 25,000 of them!) to the complex environment in which those genes work and interact. For better or worse, everything in that environment, from the meals we consume to the air we breathe to the tunes we sing (think stress or lack thereof), affects our DNA and influences how long we live.

Epigenetics, an emerging discipline of research, investigates the factors that influence genetic expression. Although genes form the vivid fabric of our being, they do not weave themselves. Our genes are the raw material ready to be weaved by a variety of biological mechanisms that control genetic behavior. These mechanisms control everything from protein synthesis to cell differentiation. They are the marching orders that tell a stem cell, "You: Go to the brain and think" or "You: Go to the spine and feel." When you consider the reality that we are all genetically diverse, the notion that any single nutrient could magically navigate and repair our particular variabilities and vulnerabilities is patently unrealistic. There's a reason Ponce de Leon never discovered his fountain of youth.

In any event, if we haven't discovered a magical food that heals the complete body, what have we found? A lot. About ten years ago, we were able to map all of the genes in the human genome. Along the way, we've discovered that practically every activity in the human body, including the development of most disease states, includes the interaction of three to more than a dozen genes. Damage to these genes can disrupt the entire process. Similar to a square dance, partners are frequently rotated to ensure a fluid performance. Consider what would happen if you slipped on a banana peel—or, more appropriately, the wrapper from some sugary junk food: the do-si-do could swiftly deteriorate into a do-sidon't.

Finally, we'll figure out how these intricate interactions interact and how to use the produce aisle to restore systemic order. For the time being, however, we are making significant progress. As researchers have learned more about the genetic, metabolic, and cellular roots of disease, they have also discovered which foods can reverse these processes. Consider cancer, which is essentially uncontrolled cell proliferation. The genetic signals that instruct cells to stop dividing have been turned off. For a long time, conventional wisdom held that once those signals were interrupted and tumor growth began, diet could do little to influence the process.

On the contrary. According to Jeanne Wallace, PhD, an expert in integrative cancer nutrition, switching from a SAD diet (the standard American diet dominated by processed foods) to a whole food diet rich in healthy fats, complex carbs, and cruciferous vegetables can restore critical signaling processes. She explains that when individuals alter their genomes, "if we do an analysis looking at hundreds of genes, we can see four hundred to five hundred oncogenes, the genes responsible for causing cancer, being turned off within a short period."

Wallace goes on to explain, "One thing I've learned from my research that has really stuck with me is that the foods we consume communicate with our genes, and we can change our gene expression through our food choices. This surprises most laypeople, who believe you're simply stuck with the genetic luck of the draw when your parents gave you birth. We've discovered that this is not true. "The expression of those inherited genes can be altered." Cooking can have numerous health benefits, as seen by this example. And when you consider how tasty certain things may be, it's not a bad pill to swallow.

So, with that introduction to how you got to be who you are today and how you can use food to affect who you become in the future (hopefully for a very long time), let's look at various physiological systems within the body and how foods can influence them for good or ill. I'm going to begin with some unsung heroes: the gut, liver, and kidney.

The Gut, Liver, and Kidneys

Although the brain and heart are typically in the forefront, I believe the gut, liver, and kidneys should be prioritized in any discussion of longevity. Perhaps they simply need a better public relations representative. Consider this: if you don't keep your body's intake and waste management systems in good working order, all of your other organs will suffer greatly. It's similar like worrying about your car's brakes when you have a blocked fuel line and a potato in the tailpipe. Forget about the brakes; the car simply will not run. No gasoline (energy) in and no exhaust (toxins) out means no go, whether for cars or people.

The Gut

The gut, or digestive tract, is where food enters, moves through, and is broken down; nutrients are absorbed; and solids are collected for evacuation. It's an extremely long and sophisticated system that begins in your mouth and travels through thirty feet of belly before reaching the final frontier. Controlling such a complex machine necessitates a clever intellect, which you fortunately possess. The enteric nervous system is located within the gut. ("Enteric" is simply a fancy way of expressing it's centered in the intestines.) Everything in the gut is coordinated by the enteric nervous system.

Neurobiologist Michael Gershon of Columbia University refers to this Grand Central Station of digestive decision making as the second brain, and for good reason: the gut has as many nerve cells as the brain, and it also contains many of the same neurotransmitters.

You've probably heard of serotonin, a neurotransmitter that influences mood, among other things. Serotonin is abundant in the gut, possibly to alert the brain when the stomach is happy—and when it is not.

Foods high in vitamin B6 (sweet potatoes and broccoli), omega-3s (wild salmon and halibut), and tryptophan (shrimp and asparagus) all help to create serotonin. In a very real sense, serotonin may play a crucial part in keeping us linked to food by providing that "gut sense" of what we require to both feel and be nourished.

How does this affect longevity? There is evidence that serotonin levels decrease as we become older. Lower serotonin levels inhibit bodily signaling between the stomach and the brain, so the body continues to request a specific food, but there isn't enough serotonin to send the message to the brain correctly. (Why do I have a cartoon of sad-faced signaling molecules in my stomach looking up and asking, "Can you hear me now?") Maintaining high serotonin levels may improve the overall signal between the two nerve systems and, as a result, assist maintain the nutritional balance required by the body. Serotonin may also assist to alleviate some forms of irritable bowel syndrome by signaling muscles to transport food further down the digestive tract.

Another source of potential stomach upset is hydrochloric acid, or HCl. You may recall HCl from high school chemistry class. Perhaps your teacher made you dress up like a mad scientist just to handle the material because it is so corrosive.

When we are young, our stomachs contain HCl, which aids in the digestion of meals. However, HCl levels fall with age. As a result, the stomach may pass food that is too intact for optimal absorption, depriving us of essential nutrients. Helicobacter pylori, a bug that causes ulcers, could be to blame. Lack of vitamin C causes H. pylori to multiply rapidly. Food can help reverse the process of impaired HCl generation caused by bacterial development.

According to Joseph Pizzorno, a naturopath who has served on medical advisory boards for presidents Bill Clinton and George W. Bush, taking 500 milligrams of vitamin C can prevent H. pylori overgrowth and promote stomach lining rebuilding, restoring hydrochloric acid production.

This book provides numerous examples of delectable foods that promote gut health. But for now, let's keep the train going and move on to the liver and kidneys.

The Liver and Kidneys

The liver and kidneys perform much of the heavy lifting in eliminating environmental poisons from our bodies. Their burden often increases as we age, due in part to the need to digest pharmaceuticals, which we use more frequently as we age.

The liver detoxifies in two steps. I won't go into the (very, very) technical details, but the key is that the liver breaks down toxins—everything from pesticides to the caffeine in your morning cup of coffee—and converts them into water-soluble molecules that can be flushed from your system rather than becoming stuck to specific fats in your tissues and potentially remaining in your body for years, wreaking havoc along the way. If the detox process is successful, the toxins will move freely through the body's liquid waterways, most commonly exiting as urine or bile.

There are numerous nutrients that keep the liver and body healthy, including one you would not expect: fiber. Heavy metals, which are mostly found in the environment, are among the end products of detoxification. If everything is working properly, the heavy metals will be transported out of the body via dietary fiber. But, as Joseph Pizzorno points out, "If you look at our evolutionary diet, we had 100 to 150 grams of fiber each day. Now, we usually consume 10 grams. We've always been exposed to heavy metals, and the body developed a way to eliminate them, but changing our diet made that mechanism much less effective."

Consuming more fiber, which is rich in foods such as whole grains, beans, berries, dark leafy greens, various crunchy vegetables, and herbs like cilantro and parsley, helps our systems remove metabolic waste from the liver, leaving our insides clean.

Another key function of certain nutrients is hydration.
According to studies, the more water we drink, the better the kidneys clear out metabolic byproducts. And thus lays the dilemma. I meet so many people who believe they are hydration failures, unable to drink the half gallon of water required for good health each day. But where is it written that all of that water must come from pure water, which not everyone enjoys? Broths and smoothies, as well as liquids like green teas, are delicious and hydrating items that can augment your water intake. Believe me, your kidneys will be just as delighted, and you'll benefit nutritionally as well.

The Brain

Many people now fear the potential mental deterioration that comes with aging more than the physical decline, and with good cause, given the increased prevalence of Alzheimer's. Memory impairment is a major concern because it can significantly reduce both quality and length of life. Fortunately, numerous nutrients can help keep your mind bright, particularly omega-3 fatty acids, which can be found in foods ranging from flaxseeds and walnuts to cold-water fish.

While the link between omega-3 consumption and brain health is well known these days, it appears that other nutritional factors may also play a significant part in the development of Alzheimer's disease, as evidenced by some fascinating studies Dr Dale Bredesen brought to my attention. Bredesen, a neurodegenerative disease expert at the University of California, San Francisco and the Buck Institute for Research on Aging, has been studying the mechanics of neurodegeneration. According to the author, individuals with type 2 diabetes, which is linked to obesity and poor diet, are twice as likely to develop Alzheimer's disease. This risk increases when insulin levels, which break down blood sugar, are raised.

Here's a probable link: high levels of the protein betaamyloid can be seen in the brains of Alzheimer's patients. Beta-amyloid is broken down and flushed out of the brain by an enzyme that also degrades insulin. Chronically high insulin levels can have negative effects on the brain due to the limited amount of insulin-degrading enzyme available.

The food cure here is twofold: cut back on refined carbs like sugar, white rice, white bread, and white pasta, and increase your intake of fiber-rich foods like whole grains, beans, and dark leafy greens. The complex carbs in these foods release sugars into the body more slowly and uniformly, and the fiber can assist decrease the absorption of sugar, both of which help maintain insulin levels stable.

Bredesen also claims that switching to unsaturated fats, such as olive oil, can help lower LDL cholesterol, lowering the risk of developing Alzheimer's. And the chef in me loves the thought that spices like curcumin and turmeric may have preventive properties as well—just another testament to the power of yum.

The Heart

Among the many discoveries about the heart, which is likely the most explored organ, are some fantastic long-term studies that have connected dietary factors to heart disease. The principles of excellent heart health are so well-known that they can be recited like a mantra: "HDL good." LDL is terrible. Triglycerides are low. High levels of aerobic activity."

Mantras are fantastic, but action is much better, which is why I always recommend foods like black beans, almonds, seeds, and wild salmon to help prevent heart disease. (Diet can help with three of the four aspects in the mantra; taking a decent walk is entirely up to you.) But what if you already have heart disease? Is there a remedy other than taking a bevy of medications? Can eating help reverse the sickness and prevent a life-threatening situation?

According to Stephen Sinatra, MD, the answer is unequivocally yes. Sinatra is an integrative cardiologist that employs diet as part of his therapeutic strategy. He practices metabolic cardiology, which involves using nutrition to improve cardiac efficiency at the cellular level, with an emphasis on mitochondria.

Mitochondria are organelles within our cells that produce energy, similar to how power plants generate electricity, except the energy mitochondria produce is in the form of adenonsine triphosphate (ATP). However, if the heart is damaged—as in congestive heart failure, a progressive condition in which the heart beats out of sync, severely impeding blood flow—the culprit could be faulty mitochondria. It's like a six-cylinder car attempting to run on five, then four, and finally just one or two cylinders. When this occurs, less ATP is produced, and Sinatra claims that "ATP is what restores cells." All of the cells in the heart have the ability to replace themselves once or twice, if not more, over their lifetime. That's why people with advanced heart disease can live for years if they receive nutritional treatment to boost their mitochondria."

Sinatra bases his nutritional support on the Awesome Foursome: coenzyme Q10 (found in wild salmon, cauliflower, and oranges), carnitine (found in grass-fed red meat, sardines, and pistachios), D-ribose (found in yogurt and mushrooms), and magnesium (found in halibut, buckwheat, and artichokes). He also recommends foods high in vitamins C and E, omega-3s, and alpha-lipoic acid (found in broccoli and spinach).

"When you build ATP, you buy time for the intrinsic stem cells within the heart to take over," says Sinatra, echoing something I've always said about spending time in the kitchen preparing health-promoting foods: how many things do you make time for that end up giving you more time back in return?

The Bones and Muscles

Along with the skin, the bones and muscles may be the most visible signs that things aren't as they used to be. We physically begin to evaporate as we age: muscle mass begins to decline by roughly 1% per year around the age of thirty, while bone density reductions frequently begin around the age of forty. The US Surgeon General's report on bone health and osteoporosis predicts that by 2030, half of all Americans will have weak bones unless we modify our food and lifestyle. The bad news is that few people take the recommended procedures to strengthen and protect their bones.

Hip fractures are a major concern for many people, particularly women, due to their serious repercussions. From a longevity standpoint, that overlooks the greater picture, which revolves around our definition of frailty. From a medical standpoint, frailty is the point on life's seesaw at which you can no longer recover from injury or sickness and instead begin what is all too often a rapid slide.

Researchers are discovering that maintaining our muscles and bones strong can help us stay vital and avoid our personal "frailty point" even as we age into our seventies, eighties, and beyond. So eat foods that promote strong and healthy bones (kale and chicken) and muscles (eggs and salmon).
It is also critical to engage in resistance exercise, such as weight lifting, even if just with very modest weights.

The Immune

System

Discussing the immune system provides an excellent opportunity to discuss antioxidants. Many cellular functions, including those of the immune system, generate waste, some of which takes the form of free radicals. If these highly reactive substances are not neutralized, they can cause a variety of negative effects, including overactivation of immune cells, which can lead to premature cell death. The immune reaction also induces inflammation, which is thought to be a precursor to a variety of illnesses, including cardiovascular disease and cancer. Abundant free radicals that maintain the immune system in permanent four-alarm fire mode may be at least largely to blame for the rising prevalence of these diseases.

Immune cells may store a high concentration of antioxidants. If you're not familiar with them, their name suggests their role: they act as a protection posse, catching predatory free radicals and preventing them from causing harm. That leads us to glutathione, which prominent physician Mark Hyman referred to as "the mother of all antioxidants, the master detoxifier and maestro of the immune system" on his Huffington Post blog.

Joseph Pizzorno concurs: "People who live the longest are the most effective at producing glutathione in the body." Certain diets encourage the production of glutathione. People who consume cysteine-rich whey diets produce more glutathione and live longer lives." Beyond whey (the watery part of milk), foods rich in cysteine, one of the three amino acids that make up glutathione, include egg yolks, asparagus, avocados, and garlic. Those foods function similarly to Pac-Man, chasing down and devouring free radical goblins.

The Respiratory System

It's a good thing I was just talking about antioxidants, because they are also important for respiratory health. Environmental toxins, including smoking, can deplete antioxidants and key nutrients, making the lungs vulnerable to diseases such as asthma, emphysema, chronic obstructive pulmonary disease (COPD), and cancer. Research on optimal lung function and nutrition is ongoing.

A review of nutrition and lung health studies published in the journal Proceedings of the Nutrition Society found that dietary choices may impact lung function and risk of common lung illnesses. In particular, a diet high in fresh fruit and fish has been linked to improved lung health."

This book emphasizes the need of eating nutrient-dense meals and getting enough antioxidants, such as vitamin C found in bell peppers, papayas, and strawberries. A large research of over a thousand adults, both smokers and nonsmokers, discovered that eating fruit on a daily basis improved lung function in both groups. So let's hear it for a kiwi every day!

The Circulatory System

You thought the gut was long at thirty feet? Think again. The circulatory system is extremely long—60,000 kilometers long. That's even longer than the United States' Interstate Highway System (47,182 miles, last I checked). Keeping all of those circulatory byways free and running is a full-time effort, and we can help by keeping our total cholesterol, particularly our LDL, or bad cholesterol, low.

People often focus on the relationship between circulation and the heart, but there are additional ways in which circulation might affect longevity. Peripheral arterial disease, which is characterized by artery obstruction in the extremities (mainly the legs), increases the risk of a heart attack or stroke. Blood flow restriction produces pain and potentially fatal blood clots. Peripheral arterial disease is more common after the age of 50, and eating can help fight it.

A study published in the Journal of Nutrition found that a combination of omega-3 fatty acids in fish oil and other nutrients helped widen blood vessels and inhibit clotting, perhaps increasing blood flow through the arteries. The researchers formulated a smoothie with fish oil, oleic acid, folic acid, vitamin B6, and vitamin E. Personally, I prefer to consume avocados (for oleic acid and vitamin B6), crunchy romaine lettuce (for folic acid), and almonds (for vitamin E). The study found that those who consumed the super shake had lower cholesterol levels and could walk twice as far before experiencing leg pain, indicating that their arteries had become more flexible, allowing for better blood flow. That is enough to make me perform a happy dance.

The Nervous System

The nervous system encompasses more than just the brain and spine. It has multiple branches and reaches all of our limbs. Peripheral nerves produce a continuous feedback loop that allows us to properly position ourselves in time and space. Consider what it would be like to weave your way along a congested city sidewalk without your nerves continually detecting where the sidewalk is. Thankfully, we don't have to constantly gaze at our feet while walking. These same nerves warn us when we're too close to harmful cold or heat, while also allowing us to enjoy the pleasure of a caress or apply exactly the proper pressure to implant a contact lens.

Keeping these nerves in good condition is not something we should take for granted. Vitamin B12 has an important role in peripheral nerve health. The University of Chicago's Center for Peripheral Neuropathy reports that a B12 deficiency "damages the myelin sheath that surrounds and protects nerves." Nerves are similar to electrical lines, and the myelin sheath serves as insulation for those lines. When the sheathing breaks down, electrical signals are disturbed. The result is peripheral neuropathy, which can produce symptoms such as tingling digits, discomfort, weakness, and an increased risk of falling.

The Endocrine System

Our bodies manufacture hormones largely through eight distinct glands called as endocrine glands. Hormones are the master controllers of our physiological functions, ranging from thyroxine, which the thyroid gland makes to boost metabolic rate, to somatotropin, or human growth hormone, which the pituitary gland generates to trigger growth spurts.

In terms of lifespan, I'd like to discuss insulin, a hormone you're probably extremely familiar with but may not be aware of. It is created deep inside the pancreas by endocrine cells known as the islets of Langerhans.

Our bodies have a love/hate relationship with insulin. It aids in the removal of excess sugar from the bloodstream, transporting it to the liver, muscles, and adipose tissue to be stored as glycogen for future use. However, if you introduce too much sugar into the bloodstream too frequently and too quickly, insulin resistance might develop. Excess sugar in the body can damage tissues, including blood vessels, leading to life-threatening conditions like diabetes.

Good dietary habits can help prevent insulin resistance. First, as previously noted in relation to Alzheimer's disease, substituting sugar and processed carbs with complex carbs and whole grains is extremely beneficial. Whole foods contain sugars, however they are typically packaged with fiber, such as a whole apple vs apple juice. Fiber slows the movement of sugar from the mouth to the bloodstream, like moguls on a slalom course. When sugars are released gradually into the bloodstream, there is less need for big doses of insulin in a short period of time.

If blood sugar is a problem for you or someone you care about, you may be aware with the glycemic index, a chart that calculates how carbohydrates in different foods may affect blood glucose levels. Glycemic load provides more valuable information because it considers the quantity of certain foods that are frequently consumed. I like to consider a meal's total carbohydrate, protein, fat, and fiber content. After all, we rarely eat food in isolation. Sure, carrots are sweet and have a high glycemic index. But don't let it discourage you from eating them. If you add a small amount of carrots to a salad with dark leafy greens, olive oil, lemon juice, fish, and nuts, the fiber in the greens, as well as the fats in the olive oil and almonds, will inhibit the release of carrot sugar into the bloodstream. As a result, the meal's overall glycemic load will be extremely low. I don't want you to miss out on the benefits of a nutrient-dense and delicious carrot due to misguided fear.

The Next Phase of the Journey

I hope you enjoyed this brief overview of the body. I know you're eager to start cooking. Before diving into the book's recipes, let's take a look at the delicious foods that belong in every longevity kitchen. The following chapter will discuss the health advantages of healthy and healing components featured in this book.

Chapter 2
The Healing Power of Food

In chapter 1, we explored how specific nutrients can improve health.

At this point, you may be wondering, "Why bother looking for the most nutritious foods and cooking so much? "Why not just take a supplement and be done with it?" It ultimately boils down to the value of team play.

What Makes Balanced Nutrition a Team Sport

The interactions of nutrients within a single diet tend to make individual nutrients easier for the body to absorb. One possible explanation is that life supports life. Foods are complex living things that, like humans, require a diverse range of nutrients to survive.

For example, consider beta-carotene. Beta-carotene-rich diets have been demonstrated to help against cancer, but at least one study found that beta-carotene supplementation had the opposite impact. Cynthia Geyer, medical director at the famed Canyon Ranch health spa in Lenox, Massachusetts, believes she understands why: "Beta-carotene does not exist in diet on its own. Apart from beta-carotene, there are at least seven more types of carotenoids. Geyer believes that their collaboration has the greatest influence on illness prevention.

Another potential aspect is the unique combination of nutrients in each dish. So, while many foods include vitamin C, for example, you may be able to obtain all of the vitamin C you require from a bell pepper, whereas my body may benefit from broccoli due to differences in our DNA and how we digest and absorb nutrients. This is the most compelling case for a diverse diet. It's another technique to change the odds in your favor. Because science has not yet evolved to tell us what our optimum foods are for acquiring the nutrients we require, bringing a variety of dishes to the table will not only keep everyone's taste buds happy, but will also increase the likelihood that each individual will receive the nutrients they require.

Supplements are sometimes essential or beneficial, but because I am, first and foremost, a cook, I prefer to supply life-enhancing nutrients through delectable cuisine wherever possible. I believe this attitude is quite impartial, and my interactions with many doctors and nutritionists support it. Many of them promote supplements solely as a temporary fix on the path to improved eating. Cindy Geyer explains, "The more I do this, the more I return to foods." If a client suffers from severe nutrition deficit, I may provide supplements to alleviate symptoms. However, this is only a temporary solution until more nutritious foods are introduced.

Colleen Fogarty Draper, MS, RD, an expert in nutrigenomics (the interaction between genes and nutrition), agrees. She believes that food is the most efficient way to deliver nutrients into the body. "You have all these bioactive components in meals that are likely to improve the absorption of any given nutrient. Our meals already have their own recipes. Consider putting just one nutrient in the body. It's like only having one flavor to eat. It's not pleasurable to consume, and it's not nourishing for the body to absorb.

Why Whole Foods Are Great Team

Players

As my amazing mentor Annemarie Colbin has often stated, if you want to know why people live so long, ask a group of genuinely seasoned folks what they've spent their entire lives eating. Colbin has done just that, and along the way she has created a lot of fascinating beliefs about food and longevity, which she has brought to the Natural Gourmet Institute for Health and Culinary Arts, a tremendously influential school she established in 1977.

Colbin, who holds a PhD in holistic nutrition, became convinced that the interplay of numerous whole foods in the body is critical to long-term health after studying science and culture from around the world. In her opinion, these dietary synergies, choreographed by seasonal shifts that keep an ever-changing patchwork of nutrition within reach, produce long-term and nutritious consequences.

I could not agree more. My entire cooking philosophy is consistent with Annemarie's. It may be summarized as follows: go to the market, get the best-looking food, preferably fresh from the farmer's field, make it taste excellent, and enjoy the repeat business. Today, we call this a whole food diet, but Grandma used to just call it "dinner."

For millennia, our species has nourished itself this way. Is it surprising that chronic diseases are on the rise now that we've moved away from eating well-balanced, whole foods? This epidemic of illness (the operative term is "epidemic") has finally sparked scientists' interest in researching how foods heal.

Science will eventually be able to explain why roasted butternut squash pairs well with dark leafy greens laced with garlic and walnuts toasted with cumin and coriander. This combination enhances nutrient absorption, potentially extending both our life span and our "health span." (In the meantime, make the Swiss Chard and Roasted Butternut Squash Tart recipe and enjoy the delightful results.) All of the pieces of this jigsaw puzzle are slowly fitting together, which excites me. But does this surprise me? No, not really. I'm first and foremost a cook. I've witnessed the delight and sense of well-being that good, nutritious foods offer to individuals who consume them. So, without further ado, let us begin getting acquainted with some of these dishes.

Chapter 3
Breakfast Recipes

Dark Chocolate Breakfast Bar

- Servings: 12 bars
- Cooking Time: 15–20 minutes
- Prep Time: 15 minutes, plus 2–3 hours cooling time

A dark chocolate breakfast bar can help activate your microbiota and stem cells, making it an excellent way to start the day.

Ingredients
- ½ cup cashews, roughly chopped (can be omitted if nut allergies)
- 2 cups old-fashioned or quick-cooking oats
- ¼ teaspoon sea salt
- ¼ cup organic dried apricots, chopped
- ¼ cup organic dried mango, chopped
- ¼ cup organic dried cranberries
- ¼ cup organic dried blueberries
- ½ cup mini dark chocolate chips (70% or greater cacao) or chopped dark chocolate
- ½ cup whole dates (approximately 6–7 large), pitted and roughly chopped
- ¼ cup maple syrup
- ½ teaspoon vanilla extract

Directions
- Preheat the oven to 350° Fahrenheit.
- In a large mixing basin, add cashews, oats, and salt. Add the apricots, mango, cranberries, blueberries, and chocolate and stir thoroughly. In a food processor, combine the dates, maple syrup, and vanilla. Puree until smooth. If the mixture is too thick or chunky, add warm water one spoonful at a time until it reaches a smooth consistency comparable to applesauce. Pour the date-maple puree over the oat and fruit mixture and stir well until everything is coated and sticky.
- Press the mixture firmly into an 8- or 9-inch square baking pan lined with parchment paper, using your fingers or the back of a spatula. Before baking, be sure to press the mixture firmly. Place on the middle rack of the oven and bake for 15-20 minutes, until the edges begin to brown. Remove and allow to cool completely

- on a cooling rack before refrigerating for 2-3 hours or overnight before cutting into individual bars. Keep covered in the fridge.

Ginger Orange Hot Chocolate

- **Servings: Four 6-ounce servings**
- **Cooking Time: 5 minutes**
- **Prep Time: 5 minutes**

Drinking hot cocoa with dark chocolate can boost your body's ability to heal by raising the number of stem cells in your blood. The most crucial component is to use dark chocolate.

Ingredients

- 3 cups almond, coconut, oat, or cows' milk
- 3 ounces (½ cup) 72% dark chocolate
- 1 ounce (¼ cup) cocoa powder
- ¼ teaspoon dried ginger or ½ teaspoon freshly grated ginger
- 1 4-inch furl of orange peel
- 1 tablespoon coconut sugar (optional)
- Whipped Coconut Cream (optional; recipe follows)

Directions

- In a small saucepan, combine the milk, chocolate, cocoa, ginger, orange peel, and, if desired, sugar. Place over medium heat and whisk until well dissolved and all chocolate has melted. Remove the orange peel and serve.
- If preferred, top with homemade whipped coconut cream.

Whipped Coconut Cream

- 1 14-ounce can coconut cream or milk
- 2 tablespoons agave syrup
- ½ teaspoon vanilla extract
- Pinch of sea salt

Directions

- Place the can of coconut cream or milk in the refrigerator overnight without shaking or tipping it, allowing the cream to separate fully from the liquid. Before whipping the next day, chill a large mixing bowl in the freezer for about 10 minutes. When ready, carefully remove the can from the fridge without disturbing it. Open the can and gently scoop out the thick, solid cream, reserving the leftover liquid for use in smoothies or drinking chocolate if desired. Transfer the thickened cream into the chilled bowl. Using an electric mixer, whip the cream for about 45 seconds until it becomes smooth. After a minute of whipping, add the agave syrup, vanilla extract, and a pinch of salt, then continue mixing until

- everything is well combined. Taste and adjust sweetness if needed.
- The whipped coconut cream can be used immediately or stored in the refrigerator, where it will firm up further. It will stay fresh for up to one week.

Warm Carrot Top Salad

- Servings: 4
- Cooking Time: 15 minutes
- Prep Time: 15 minutes

A warm salad with cumin, antiangiogenic carrot tips, shiitake mushrooms, and cherry tomatoes.

Ingredients
- 1 bunch carrot tops, tender leaves chopped into 1–2-inch lengths; discard tough stems
- 2 tablespoons extra virgin olive oil, plus more for garnish
- ½ medium onion, diced
- 2 cloves garlic, minced
- 1 cup shiitake mushrooms caps and stems, thinly sliced
- ½ teaspoon sea salt, plus more for garnish
- ½ teaspoon crushed red pepper flakes (optional)
- ½ teaspoon ground cumin
- 1 cup cherry tomatoes, halved
- Grated zest of one lemon
- Freshly ground black pepper, to taste

Directions
- Place the carrot tops on a big serving bowl or tray and leave aside.
- In a sauté pan, heat the olive oil over medium-high heat. Cook the onion and garlic until transparent, aromatic, and faintly golden brown, about 2-3 minutes. Cook the mushrooms for an additional 3-5 minutes, or until tender. Season with sea salt, red pepper flakes (if using), and cumin. Sauté the tomatoes until softened. Toss cooked vegetables with carrot tops and wilted leaves. Season with salt, pepper, lemon zest, and a drizzle of extra virgin olive oil. Serve immediately.

Classic Lemon Vinaigrette Dressing

- Servings: 4–6
- Cooking Time: 0 minutes
- Prep Time: 5 minutes

Salads can be created with various greens, herbs, and vegetables. Choosing the correct dressing may elevate a salad from mediocre to great. Salads can be readily customized using healthful ingredients from the list.

Ingredients
- 1 small clove garlic, minced
- 1 salt-packed anchovy, rinsed
- ½ lemon, juiced
- 1 teaspoon Dijon mustard
- ¼ cup extra virgin olive oil
- Freshly cracked black pepper, to taste
- Sea salt, to taste

Directions
- To make a paste, combine garlic and anchovies in a mortar and pestle or small basin using a spoon. Mix in the lemon juice and mustard. Pour in the olive oil and whisk to combine the ingredients.
- Add some freshly ground black pepper to taste. Add a pinch of salt. If you bring your lunch to work, you can store the dressing in a jar and pour it over your salad throughout the meal.

Roasted Mushrooms

- **Servings: 4**
- **Cooking Time: 30 minutes**
- **Prep Time: 10 minutes**

This combination of immune-boosting mushrooms benefits both your microbiome and your angiogenesis defenses.

Ingredients
- 2 pounds mushrooms (white button, shiitake, cremini, chanterelle, morel, maitake, and/or porcini), both caps and stems, cleaned and thickly sliced on the diagonal
- ¼ cup extra virgin olive oil
- 4 cloves garlic, minced
- Freshly cracked black pepper, to taste
- 6–8 sprigs of thyme or rosemary
- Sea salt, to taste
- 1 sprig Italian parsley, finely chopped

Directions
- Preheat the oven to 450° F. In a large mixing bowl, add the mushrooms, olive oil, garlic, and black pepper and gently whisk. Spread the mushroom mixture evenly on a large parchment-lined baking sheet or roasting pan, then top with thyme sprigs and bake. Roast for 25-30 minutes, until the mushrooms are golden brown. Allow to cool somewhat, then season with salt, put chopped parsley over top, and serve warm.
- **Note:** It is not recommended to wash or soak mushrooms in water. To clean them, use a wet paper towel or

kitchen towel to delicately wipe them. Do not add salt to the mushrooms until they are done cooking.

Grilled Eggplant

- **Servings: 4–6**
- **Grilling Time: 5–6 minutes**
- **Prep Time: 20 minutes, minimum 30 minutes rest time**

Eggplant contains chlorogenic acid, which boosts your regenerative system and health defenses. This recipe involves grilling the meat first and then dressing it with health-boosting spices that add taste and bioactives to the flesh, resulting in a delicious and nutritious meal.

Ingredients
- 4 small or 2 medium eggplants
- 2 teaspoons fresh oregano, chopped, or 1 teaspoon dried oregano
- Large bunch fresh mint leaves, chopped (can use parsley if preferred)
- 3–4 cloves garlic, finely chopped
- Salt, to taste
- Crushed red pepper flakes, to taste (optional)
- ¼ cup extra virgin olive oil
- Good-quality balsamic vinegar, to taste
- 6–8 basil leaves
- Chopped olives, to taste (optional)
- Capers, to taste (optional)

Directions
- Preheat an outdoor or stovetop grill. Wash and dry the eggplants. Remove the top and bottom ends. Cut the eggplant in ¼-inch lengthwise slices.
- Grill the eggplant slices for 2–3 minutes per side. When the eggplant has finished cooking, arrange it in a single layer in a large casserole dish. Garnish with oregano, mint, garlic, salt, and red pepper flakes, if using. Drizzle with olive oil. Top with a little drizzle of balsamic vinegar. Continue with up to three layers of eggplant and seasonings.
- Cover firmly with plastic wrap and let sit at room temperature or in the fridge for at least 30 minutes to allow all of the flavors to saturate the eggplant. This dish can also be prepared ahead of time and refrigerated overnight, or it can be kept in the fridge in a firmly sealed container for 7-10 days.
- To serve, place the eggplant slices on a serving plate and top with basil leaves, either whole or julienned. Optional garnishes include olives and/or capers.
- This recipe works well as an appetizer or side dish, or as a salad with arugula. Before serving, chop the eggplant into bite-sized pieces and serve with toasted bread as bruschetta.

Broccoli Stem and Oregano Soup

- **Serves: 6–8**
- **Cooking Time: 20 minutes**
- **Prep Time: 10 minutes**

Incorporating broccoli stems and florets into your diet can help reduce angiogenesis. This recipe includes broccoli sprouts to enhance the immune system.

Ingredients
- 1 head broccoli
- 2 tablespoons extra virgin olive oil
- 1 medium yellow onion, peeled and chopped
- 4 cloves garlic, finely chopped
- 2 teaspoons dried oregano
- 5 cups vegetable broth
- 2 cups spinach, rinsed
- 1 cup flat-leaf parsley, rinsed with the stems removed
- Zest of ½ lemon
- Kosher salt, to taste
- Freshly ground black pepper, to taste
- Broccoli sprouts (for garnish; optional)

Directions
- Set aside the broccoli florets after removing them from the stalk. Remove the bark from the broccoli stems and slice into 1-inch cubes. Keep the florets and stems separated.
- Heat the olive oil in a big pot over medium-high heat. Cook the onions and garlic for about 5 minutes, or until they are transparent and fragrant.
- Sauté the chopped broccoli stems and oregano for 3-5 minutes before adding the veggie broth. Bring to a boil, then lower to a simmer over medium heat for 10 minutes, or until the broccoli is soft. Set aside.
- Heat 4 cups of water in a medium pot till boiling. Blanch the broccoli florets for 2-3 minutes, then quickly transfer to an ice bath to chill. Repeat this procedure with the parsley and spinach, and then pat them dry with a paper towel or kitchen towel.
- Place the broccoli stem broth combination in a blender and blend on medium-high speed. Slowly add the drained broccoli, spinach, and parsley, then blend on high until smooth and vivid green. Season to taste with salt and pepper, then garnish with lemon zest and broccoli sprouts.

Chestnut Soup

- **Servings: 4**
- **Cooking Time: 30 minutes**
- **Prep Time: 10 minutes**

This soup is a fantastic way to acquire ellagic acid from chestnuts and is a comforting fall dish. Serve this with sautéed mushrooms and crusty sourdough bread.

Ingredients
- 2 tablespoons extra virgin olive oil, plus more for garnish
- 1 large shallot, chopped
- 2 ribs of celery with leafy tops, chopped
- 1 medium carrot, chopped
- 1 clove garlic, chopped
- 2 sprigs thyme, leaves picked
- 3 fresh or 1 dried bay leaf, left whole to be removed later
- Sea salt, to taste
- Black pepper, to taste
- 1½ cups cooked chestnuts
- 4 cups vegetable stock

Directions
- Using a medium-sized pot, warm the extra virgin olive oil over medium-high heat. Sauté shallot, celery, carrots, garlic, thyme, bay leaf, salt, and pepper until aromatic, approximately 5-7 minutes. Stir in the chestnuts until fully combined. Add the veggie stock and bring to a boil. Then lower the heat and let it cook for 20 minutes on medium-low. Remove all bay leaves. Process the soup with an immersion blender until creamy and smooth. Add salt and pepper to taste. Add a little extra virgin olive oil to bowls of soup to make them look nice.

Mushroom Soup

- **Servings: 4**
- **Cooking Time: 30 minutes**
- **Prep Time: 10 minutes**

This warm and cozy soup can be made with a variety of immune boosting mushrooms that provide rich umami qualities. Experiment with different types of mushrooms using this basic recipe.

Ingredients
- 2 tablespoons extra virgin olive oil
- 1 large shallot, chopped
- 4 cloves garlic, minced
- 1 pound mushrooms (button, shiitake, chanterelle, cremini, and/or oyster), chopped
- 3–4 sprigs thyme, leaves picked
- Sea salt, to taste
- 4 cups vegetable stock
- Black pepper, to taste
- ¼ cup Italian parsley, chopped

Directions
- In a medium saucepan, heat olive oil over medium-high heat and sauté shallot and garlic until aromatic (4-5 minutes). Season with sea salt after adding mushrooms and thyme leaves to the dish. Sauté till golden brown,

approximately 4-5 minutes. Set aside a few decorative mushroom pieces to decorate the soup before serving. Add stock and simmer for another 15-20 minutes. Smooth up the soup with an immersion blender or normal blender. Season with salt and pepper to taste. Garnish with the saved mushrooms and minced parsley.

Pumpkin Soup

- **Servings: 4**
- **Cooking Time: 45 minutes**
- **Prep Time: 10 minutes**

This classic autumn soup uses pumpkins, also known as potimarron in Europe.

Ingredients
- 2–3 small sugar pumpkins, or 2 cups organic pumpkin puree (2 15-ounce cans)
- 2–3 tablespoons extra virgin olive oil
- Sea salt, to taste
- 2 cloves garlic, chopped
- 1 medium white onion, chopped
- ¼ teaspoon black pepper
- ½ teaspoon cardamom
- ½ teaspoon cinnamon
- ½ teaspoon turmeric
- ¼ teaspoon nutmeg
- 2 cups vegetable stock
- 1 cup coconut milk
- Pumpkin seeds, to taste

Directions
- Turn on the oven to 350°F and line a baking sheet with parchment paper. Cut the pumpkins in half and scoop out the seeds and threads. Drizzle with extra virgin olive oil, sprinkle with sea salt, and arrange face down on a baking pan. Bake the pumpkins for 30-45 minutes, or until a knife can easily be inserted into their flesh. Wait for them to cool before peeling. Set aside.
- In a medium pot, bring the olive oil to a medium-high heat. Add the onion and garlic to the pan, season with pepper and ¼ teaspoon of salt, and cook for about 2 to 3 minutes, until the flavor is nice. Stir in the cardamom, cinnamon, turmeric, and nutmeg until thoroughly combined. Mix in the pumpkin flesh until thoroughly coated and combined. Simmer the stock and coconut milk until hot and bubbly. The soup should be smooth and creamy after being processed with an immersion blender. Season to taste with sea salt. Garnish with pumpkin seeds.

Roasted Purple Potato Soup

- **Servings: 4**

- **Cooking Time: 45 minutes**
- **Prep Time: 10 minutes**

Potato soup has never tasted so wonderful. Purple potatoes contain a natural color that kills cancer stem cells and inhibits angiogenesis. To support your microbiome, serve this soup with a dollop of yogurt.

Ingredients

- 1 pound (4–6 medium) purple potatoes, peeled and cut into 1-inch pieces
- 3 tablespoons extra virgin olive oil, divided
- Sea salt, to taste
- Freshly ground black pepper
- ½ small red onion or 1 large shallot, diced
- 2 cloves garlic, minced
- 1 rib celery with leafy top, chopped
- 2 small stalks rosemary, left whole for removal later
- 4–6 cups vegetable broth
- Finely chopped parsley or dill
- Yogurt (for garnish; optional)

Directions

- Warm the oven up to 400°F. Put the potatoes on a big baking sheet that is either nonstick or has parchment paper or nonstick foil on it. Sprinkle with salt and pepper and 1 tablespoon of the extra virgin olive oil. For about 25 to 30 minutes, roast the potatoes until they start to turn brown and get soft.
- Put the last two tablespoons of olive oil in a medium-sized stockpot and heat it over medium-high heat. Put in the onion and cook for one to two minutes. Add the rosemary, garlic, and celery. Season with salt and pepper. Sauté for about 4 to 5 minutes, until the vegetables are soft and smell good. After the potatoes are done cooking, add enough broth to cover them completely. Bring to a boil, then lower the heat and let it cook for 8 to 10 minutes, until the potatoes are soft. Take the rosemary stalks off and throw them away. Blend the soup with an immersion blender until it is smooth and creamy. As needed, add sea salt. Add freshly ground black pepper and chopped parsley or dill on top.
- If you're using yogurt, add a big amount of it on top of the soup.

Basic Pesto with Trofie

- **Servings: 2–3**
- **Cooking Time: 0 minutes**
- **Prep Time: 5 minutes**

This classic pasta from Liguria, Italy, tastes great, is easy to make, and has a special mix of bioactives from the pine nuts, garlic, olive oil, and basil. Chestnut flour is often used to make the pasta, which gives it an extra healthy twist.

Ingredients

- 2 cups fresh basil leaves, stems removed
- ¼ cup pine nuts or walnuts
- 2 small cloves garlic
- ⅔ cup extra virgin olive oil, divided
- ⅔ cup grated Parmigiano-Reggiano cheese, plus more for garnish
- Sea salt, to taste
- 1 pound trofie pasta, made with chestnut flour (can be ordered online if your market does not carry it)

Directions

- In a food processor, blend the basil, almonds, garlic, oil, and cheese. Pulse to combine thoroughly. Pour the remaining olive oil into the processor gently and steadily. When fully integrated, stop processing and transfer to a bowl. Fold in the remainder of the cheese. To taste, add a pinch of sea salt.
- Meanwhile, heat a big pot of salted water to a boil. Cook the pasta until al dente, about 1 minute less than the package guidelines. Before straining pasta in a strainer, set aside 1 cup of the cooking water. In a large serving bowl, combine pasta, pesto, and enough cooking water to evenly coat. Serve immediately, garnished with more Parmigiano-Reggiano.

Chapter 4
Life-Enhancing Soups and Broths

Magic Mineral Broth 2.0

- **Prep: 10 min**
- **Cook: 2–4 hrs**
- **Storage: Fridge 6 days / Freezer 4 months**

I perfected Magic Mineral Broth after a year of testing—it's a nutrient-rich, delicious veggie broth. In this book, I've upgraded it with fennel and thyme for even greater health and longevity benefits.

Ingredients
- 1 fennel bulb, with tops
- 2 unpeeled yellow onions, cut into quarters
- 6 unpeeled carrots, cut into thirds
- 1 leek, white and green parts, cut into thirds
- 1 bunch celery, including the heart, cut into thirds
- 2 unpeeled sweet potatoes, cut into chunks
- 1 unpeeled garnet yam, cut into chunks
- 1 large bunch fresh flat-leaf parsley
- 6 sprigs fresh thyme
- 12 large cloves unpeeled garlic, smashed
- 1 (3-inch) piece of unpeeled fresh ginger, cut in half lengthwise
- 1 (8-inch) strip of kombu
- 12 black peppercorns
- 4 juniper berries or allspice berries
- 2 bay leaves
- 8 quarts cold filtered water, plus more if needed
- 1 teaspoon sea salt

Directions
- Rinse the vegetables thoroughly, including the kombu. Combine the fennel, onions, carrots, leek, celery, sweet potatoes, yam, parsley, thyme, garlic, ginger, kombu, peppercorns, juniper berries, and bay leaves in a 12-quart or larger stockpot. Pour in the water, cover, and bring to a boil over high heat. Reduce the heat to low and cook uncovered for 2 to 4 hours. As the broth simmers, some of the water will evaporate; add extra if the vegetables start to peek through. Simmer until the vegetables'

- full richness is tasted.
- Using a big, coarse-mesh sieve set over a large heat-safe container, strain the broth. Stir in the salt. Allow to cool to room temperature before storing in the refrigerator or freezer.
- To improve immunity, try adding 8 entire shiitake mushrooms, 1 (6-inch) piece of burdock root (washed and cut into quarters), or both.

Chicken Magic Mineral Broth 2.0

- **Prep: 10 min**
- **Cook: 2–4 hrs**
- **Storage: Fridge 6 days / Freezer 4 months**

Magic Mineral Broth gets even better by simmering chicken bones to pull out nutrients that support cartilage, immune cells, blood, and bones. Plus, the bones make it even more flavorful.

Ingredients
- 1 fennel bulb, with tops
- 2 unpeeled yellow onions, cut into quarters
- 6 unpeeled carrots, cut into thirds
- 1 leek, white and green parts, cut into thirds
- 1 bunch celery, including the heart, cut into thirds
- 2 unpeeled sweet potatoes, cut into chunks
- 1 unpeeled garnet yam, cut into chunks
- 1 large bunch fresh flat-leaf parsley
- 6 sprigs fresh thyme
- 12 large cloves unpeeled garlic, smashed
- 1 (3-inch) piece of unpeeled fresh ginger, cut in half lengthwise
- 1 (8-inch) strip of kombu
- 12 black peppercorns
- 4 juniper berries or allspice berries
- 2 bay leaves
- 1 tablespoon vinegar or freshly squeezed lemon juice
- 1 organic chicken carcass, or 2 pounds organic chicken bones
- 8 quarts cold filtered water, plus more if needed
- 1 teaspoon sea salt

Directions
- Rinse the vegetables thoroughly, including the kombu. Place the fennel, onions, carrots, leek, celery, sweet potatoes, yam, parsley, thyme, garlic, ginger, kombu, peppercorns, juniper berries, bay leaves, vinegar, and chicken carcass in a 12-quart or larger stockpot. Add the water, put the lid on top, and heat it up to a high level. Reduce the heat to low and cook uncovered for 2 to 4 hours. Some of the water will evaporate while the soup simmers; add more if the vegetables start to peek through.

- Simmer until the vegetables are fully rich in flavor.
- Strain the broth through a large, coarse-mesh sieve set over a big, heatproof container. Stir in the salt. Allow to cool to room temperature before storing overnight in the refrigerator. Skim off as much fat from the top of the broth as possible, then transfer to airtight containers and chill or freeze.
- To improve immunity, try adding 8 entire shiitake mushrooms, 1 (6-inch) piece of burdock root (washed and cut into quarters), or both.

Chilled Curried Cucumber Soup

- **Prep: 10 min**
- **Cook: 2 hrs (chilling)**
- **Storage: Fridge 5 days**

Yogurt, rich in live cultures, supports digestion, fights infection, and stars in dishes from breads to smoothies. In this refreshing soup, yogurt blends with cucumber, garlic, spices, and herbs for a taste of summer and tradition.

Ingredients
- 2¼ cups organic plain yogurt
- 1 pound, 4 ounces English cucumbers, peeled, seeded, and chopped
- 1 teaspoon minced fresh ginger
- ½ teaspoon chopped garlic
- 1¼ teaspoons curry powder
- ½ teaspoon sea salt
- ½ teaspoon ground cumin
- 2 teaspoons freshly squeezed lemon
- 1 teaspoon grated lemon zest
- 1 tablespoon chopped fresh mint

Directions
- Combine yogurt, cucumbers, ginger, garlic, curry powder, salt, cumin, lemon juice, and lemon zest in a blender and pulse until smooth. Taste and add up to ¾ teaspoon of salt.
- Transfer to a glass container, cover, and chill for at least 2 hours. Just before serving, add the mint.

Velvety Mediterranean Gazpacho with Avocado Cream

- **Prep: 20 min**
- **Storage:**
- **- Gazpacho: Fridge 5 days / Freezer 1 month**
- **- Avocado Cream: Fridge 2 days (with lemon/lime spritz)**

Instead of tequila, I sip this Mediterranean gazpacho—a vibrant blend of veggies like cucumbers, peppers, and tomatoes. Just chop, blend, and serve; it's easy, refreshing, and always a hit at parties.

Ingredients

AVOCADO CREAM WITH BASIL
- 1 avocado, halved and flesh scooped out
- 2 tablespoons water
- 2 teaspoons coarsely chopped fresh basil
- ¾ teaspoon freshly squeezed lemon juice
- ⅛ teaspoon sea salt

GAZPACHO
- 3 cups low-sodium tomato juice
- ¼ cup extra-virgin olive oil
- 1 tablespoon plus 1 teaspoon freshly squeezed lemon juice
- 1 tablespoon Grade B maple syrup
- 1 teaspoon sea salt
- ½ teaspoon ground cumin
- ¼ teaspoon ground coriander
- ⅛ teaspoon cayenne
- 2 cloves garlic, coarsely chopped
- 1 fennel bulb, cut into quarters and cored
- 3 celery stalks, coarsely chopped
- 1 English cucumber, peeled, seeded, and coarsely chopped
- 1 red bell pepper, seeded and coarsely chopped
- 2 cups cherry tomatoes
- 1 small red onion, coarsely chopped
- ¼ cup coarsely chopped fresh basil, cilantro, or a combination

Directions
- To prepare the avocado cream, combine all of the ingredients and mix until very smooth. Transfer the mixture to a small bowl. (There is no need to rinse the blender before starting.)
- To create the gazpacho, combine all of the ingredients in a large basin and whisk well. Working in batches, pour to the blender and puree until absolutely smooth. Taste; you might want to add some salt or maple syrup. Pour the mixture into small glasses and top with avocado cream.

Summer's Sweetest Corn Bisque

- **Prep: 20 min**
- **Cook: 40 min**
- **Storage: Fridge 5 days / Freezer 4 months**

Fresh corn is packed with phytonutrients and incredible flavor, unlike processed corn products. In this soup, shaved cobs create a rich broth and sweet, summery taste that lingers like a sunset.

Ingredients
- 12 ears of corn
- 10 cups filtered water
- Sea salt
- 2 tablespoons extra-virgin olive oil
- 2 cups diced yellow onions
- Chive Oil, for garnish

Directions
- Take the corn kernels off and set them away. Put the corncobs, water, and 2½ teaspoons of salt in a big pot that is set over medium-low heat. Put the lid on and cook for 30 minutes.
- Put the olive oil in a big skillet and heat it over medium-low heat. Put in the onions and a lot of salt. Cook for about 7 minutes, until the onions turn brown. Put in the corn kernels and a lot of salt. Sauté for another 4 minutes, or until the corn is just barely soft.
- Take the corncobs out of the pot and throw them away. Pour some of the water into a blender at a time. Put in some of the corn mixture and process until it's very smooth. For a smooth texture, strain each batch through a fine-mesh sieve, pressing it with the back of a spoon to get out as much liquid as you can. Put the soup back in the pot and add a little salt. Warm up on low heat until it's just right. Serve with a drizzle of Chive Oil on top.
- Optional: Set aside 1 cup of the corn and onion blend to make a chunky chowder. The soup is now smooth. Add the corn and onions that you saved, along with ¼ cup of peeled and diced carrot, ¼ cup of diced celery, and ½ cup of diced red potatoes. Simmer on low heat for about 8 minutes, turning every now and then, until the carrots and potatoes are just barely soft.

Costa Rican Black Bean Soup with Sweet Potato

- **Prep: 20 min (after soaking)**
- **Cook: 1 hr 30 min**
- **Storage: Fridge 5 days / Freezer 2 months**

Costa Ricans, known for longevity, grow up eating fiber-rich black beans and sweet potatoes packed with phytochemicals. This dish blends their vibrant flavors with cayenne, cinnamon, cumin, and garlic for a true taste of paradise.

Ingredients
- 2 tablespoons extra-virgin olive oil
- 2 cups diced yellow onions
- Sea salt

- 1½ teaspoons seeded and finely diced jalapeño chile
- 1 tablespoon minced garlic
- 1½ teaspoons dried oregano
- ½ teaspoon ground cumin
- ¼ teaspoon ground cinnamon
- Pinch of cayenne
- 8 cups vegetable broth, homemade or store-bought
- 2 cups dried black beans, soaked, rinsed, and drained
- 1 (6-inch) strip of kombu
- 1 cinnamon stick
- 1 bay leaf
- 2 cups finely diced orange-fleshed sweet potato, such as garnet yams
- 2 teaspoons freshly squeezed lime juice
- ¼ cup chopped fresh cilantro, for garnish
- Ancho Chile Relish, for garnish

Directions

- The olive oil should be heated in a soup pot over medium heat. Put in the onions and a pinch of salt. Sauté for about 4 minutes, until the onions are clear. Sauté the jalapeños, garlic, oregano, cumin, cinnamon, cayenne, and ¼ teaspoon salt for 1 minute. Pour ½ cup of broth to deglaze the pot, stirring to dislodge any stuck particles. Cook until liquid has been reduced by half. Put in the last 7½ cups of broth along with the bay leaf, cinnamon stick, kombu, and black beans. Push the heat all the way up and boil it. Lower the heat to medium-low, cover slightly, and simmer quickly (bubbles should form on the surface often) for about 1 hour and 15 minutes, or until the beans are soft.
- Add the sweet potato and ¼ teaspoon of salt and mix well. It will take about 7 minutes of simmering with the lid on until the sweet potato is just soft. Take out the kombu, cinnamon stick, and bay leaf with an angled spoon and throw them away. Put 2 cups of the beans and sweet potatoes into a blender. Blend them until the mixture is very smooth. Return the combined mixture to the soup and simmer just until heated through. Add the lime juice and mix it in. Then do a FASS check. You might need to add ¼ teaspoon of salt and a spritz of lime juice. Put some parsley and Ancho Chile Relish on top of the dish before serving.

Dahl Fit for a Saint

- **Prep: 15 min**
- **Cook: 45 min**
- **Storage: Fridge 5 days / Freezer 2 months**

At the Chopra Center, I learned that spices can be the heart of a dish, not just an add-on. This dahl, rich in healing spices, earned a saint's smile and taught me the true power of flavor and nutrition.

Ingredients

- 2 tablespoons organic ghee or extra-virgin olive oil
- 1½ teaspoons cumin seeds
- 1½ teaspoons black or brown mustard seeds
- 1 yellow onion, diced small
- 1 tablespoon minced fresh ginger
- 2 teaspoons turmeric
- 2 teaspoons ground cumin
- Sea salt
- 2 cups chopped tomatoes, or 1 (14.5-ounce) can diced tomatoes, drained and juices reserved
- 8 cups vegetable broth, homemade or store-bought
- 2 cups dried red lentils, rinsed well
- 1 cinnamon stick
- 3 cups loosely packed baby spinach
- 1 teaspoon freshly squeezed lime juice
- ½ teaspoon Grade B maple syrup
- ¼ cup finely chopped fresh cilantro or mint, for garnish

Directions

- In a soup saucepan, cook the ghee over medium heat. Add the cumin and mustard seeds and cook until they start to explode. Sauté the onion, ginger, turmeric, ground cumin, and a bit of salt for about 3 minutes. Sauté the drained tomatoes with ¼ teaspoon salt for 2 minutes. To deglaze the pot, add ½ cup of broth and the leftover tomato juice. Stir to release any stuck bits. Cook until liquid has been reduced by half. Stir in the lentils, followed by the remaining 7½ cups of liquid and the cinnamon stick. Turn up the heat to high and bring to a boil. Reduce the heat to low, cover, and cook for approximately 30 minutes, or until the lentils are cooked.
- Add ¼ teaspoon salt and boil for 5 minutes. Remove the cinnamon stick, then combine the spinach, lime juice, and maple syrup. Serve with a garnish of cilantro.

Rustic Lentil Soup

- **Prep: 20 min**
- **Cook: 40 min**
- **Storage: Fridge 5 days / Freezer 3 months**

Inspired by my dad's creative spirit, this hearty lentil soup evolved from a red wine–braised dish into a rich, satisfying bowl. Packed with lentils, mushrooms, Swiss chard, and spices, it's as healthy as it is delicious.

Ingredients

- 2 tablespoons extra-virgin olive oil
- 1 yellow onion, diced small
- Sea salt

- 2 carrots, peeled and diced small
- 2 celery stalks, diced small
- 1 cup finely diced parsnips
- 8 ounces cremini mushrooms, sliced
- 1 tablespoon minced garlic
- ½ teaspoon dried thyme
- ½ teaspoon dried oregano
- ¼ teaspoon freshly ground black pepper
- 1 cup red wine
- 2 tablespoons tomato paste
- 1 (14.5-ounce) can diced tomatoes
- 1 cup dried green lentils, rinsed well
- 7 cups vegetable broth, homemade or store-bought
- 1 bay leaf
- 2½ cups stemmed and chopped Swiss chard, in bite-size pieces

Directions

- In a large skillet set over medium heat, heat the olive oil. Sauté the onion with a pinch of salt until transparent, about 4 minutes. Sauté the carrot, celery, parsnips, mushrooms, and another pinch of salt for 12 minutes, or until the veggies are soft and deep golden brown.
- Sauté garlic for 30 seconds. Stir in thyme, oregano, pepper, and ¼ teaspoon salt. Pour in the wine to deglaze the skillet, swirling to release any particles stuck to the bottom. Cook until liquid has been reduced by half. Mix in the tomato paste, tomatoes, and lentils. Add the broth and bay leaf. Increase the heat to high and bring to a boil. Reduce the heat to low, cover, and simmer for approximately 20 minutes, or until the lentils are cooked. Taste; you may add a spritz of lemon juice or a teaspoon of salt. Stir in the Swiss chard and cook for 3 minutes, or until tender.
- Variations: Replace the celery with fennel, which is a wonderful digestive aid, to add depth to the flavor. If you are not a fan of mushrooms, simply leave them out. You can use 1 cup of broth instead of wine.

Ridiculously Good Split Pea Soup

- **Prep: 15 min**
- **Cook: 1 hr**
- **Storage: Fridge 3 days**

This velvety split pea soup, loved instantly by my assistant Katie ("OMG!"), blends peas, garlic, carrots, onions, and thyme into a fiber-rich, smoky dish. It's hearty, healthy, and full of flavor—with or without the optional smoky twist.

Ingredients

- 2 tablespoons extra-virgin olive oil
- 1 cup finely diced yellow onion

- Sea salt
- 1 cup peeled and finely diced carrot
- ½ cup finely diced celery
- ¼ teaspoon dried thyme
- Freshly ground black pepper
- 2 cloves garlic, minced
- 2 cups dried green split peas, rinsed well
- 8 cups vegetable broth, homemade or store-bought
- 2 teaspoons freshly squeezed lemon juice
- 1 tablespoon finely chopped fresh flat-leaf parsley, for garnish
- Chive Oil, for garnish

Directions

- In a medium-sized soup saucepan, heat the olive oil. Sauté the onion with a pinch of salt until golden, about 8 minutes. Sauté the carrot, celery, thyme, ¼ teaspoon salt, and ⅛ teaspoon pepper for approximately 8 minutes. Stir in garlic and split peas, then pour in ½ cup of broth to deglaze the saucepan. Stir to dislodge any stuck parts. Cook until the liquid has been reduced by half. Add the remaining 7 ½ cups of broth. Increase the heat to high and bring to a boil. Reduce the heat to low and simmer for approximately 40 minutes, or until the split peas are soft.
- Place 2 cups of the soup in a blender and mix until velvety smooth. Stir the combined ingredients back into the soup and cook until heated through. Mix in lemon juice, ¼ teaspoon salt, and pepper. Conduct a FASS test; you may wish to add a spritz of lemon juice and a pinch of salt. Garnished with the chives and parsley.
- To add a smokey taste, sauté the onion with ¼ teaspoon smoked paprika or 2 dried chipotle chilies, rehydrated and chopped.

Chapter 5
Vital Vegetables

Avocado Lover's Salad

- **Prep: 5 min**
- **Cook: N/A**
- **Storage: Fridge 5 days**

My brother begged me for "avotatoes," but instead, I created this dish to showcase avocado's rich flavor, creamy texture, and powerful anti-aging benefits. Packed with healthy fats and antioxidants, it's a true superfood treat.

Ingredients
- 1 head romaine lettuce, torn into bite-size pieces (about 8 cups)
- 1 English cucumber, peeled, seeded, and diced
- 1 red bell pepper, diced
- Greener Than Green Goddess Dressing
- 1 large avocado, diced
- ¼ cup pumpkin seeds, toasted
- 2 tablespoons chopped fresh mint
- 2 teaspoons chopped fresh cilantro

Directions
- To prepare, combine lettuce, cucumber, and bell pepper in a big bowl. Drizzle with dressing and toss one more. Add avocado, pumpkin seeds, mint, and cilantro and toss again.

Carrot Apple Slaw with Cranberries

- **Prep: 15 min**
- **Storage: Fridge 3 days**

Unlike heavy classic slaws, this vibrant mix of carrots, cranberries, apples, and mint is a feast for the eyes and palate. Crisp, chewy, tart, and sweet, it's as healthy as it is beautiful.

Ingredients
- ¼ cup unsweetened dried cranberries
- ¼ cup very thinly sliced red onion
- 3 tablespoons freshly squeezed orange juice
- 1 tablespoon freshly squeezed lemon juice

- 8 ounces carrots, peeled and thinly sliced into ¼-inch strips
- 1 Granny Smith apple, thinly sliced into ¼-inch strips
- 1 tablespoon chopped fresh mint
- ¼ teaspoon sea salt
- 2 tablespoons extra-virgin olive oil
- 1 tablespoon slivered almonds, toasted

Directions

- In a separate bowl, mix together the cranberries, onion, 1 tablespoon orange juice, and lemon juice. Allow to settle for a few minutes so that the fluids may penetrate the cranberries and onion.
- Toss the carrots, apple, mint, salt, cranberry combination, and remaining 2 tablespoons orange juice in a large bowl to blend. Drizzle with olive oil and toss again. Sprinkle the almonds on top.
- Feel free to add ⅓ cup of fresh or frozen shelled edamame mixed with a little lemon juice and sea salt, or you can add 1 cup of finely shred cabbage. Instead of red onion, use scallions.

Mexican Cabbage Crunch

- **Prep: 20 min**
- **Storage: Fridge 5 days**

Crunchy cabbage and jicama team up with cilantro, jalapeños, pumpkin seeds, and a zesty cumin-lime vinaigrette for a fresh, healthy bite. It's so irresistible, you won't stop at one bowl.

Ingredients

- 6 cups shredded red cabbage
- 4 cups julienned jicama
- ½ cup finely chopped fresh cilantro
- 1 tablespoon seeded and diced jalapeño chile (optional)
- ½ cup of Lime Vinaigrette with Toasted Cumin Seeds
- ½ cup pumpkin seeds, toasted

Directions

- Toss the cabbage, jicama, cilantro, and jalapeño in a large bowl until well combined. Drizzle with dressing and toss one more. Wait a few minutes for the dressing to penetrate the cabbage.
- Sprinkle the pumpkin seeds on top immediately before serving.

Asian Cabbage Crunch

- **Prep: 20 min**
- **Storage: Fridge 2 days**

Red cabbage, often overlooked, is packed with anti-inflammatory and antibacterial nutrients. It even helps the liver break down excess estrogen, making it a powerful food for longevity and wellness.

Ingredients

- 3 cups shredded red cabbage
- 3 cups shredded Napa cabbage
- 1 cup thinly sliced red bell pepper
- 3 scallions, white and green parts, thinly sliced
- ¼ cup finely chopped fresh cilantro or basil
- 2 tablespoons finely chopped fresh mint
- ½ cup Sesame Miso Dressing
- 1 tablespoon black sesame seeds

Directions

- In a large bowl, add the cabbages, bell pepper, onions, cilantro, and mint. Drizzle with dressing and toss until well coated. Sprinkle with sesame seeds and let aside for a few minutes to enable the dressing to absorb into the cabbage.
- Variation: Mix in 1 cup of fresh or frozen shelled edamame, a spritz of lime juice, and a teaspoon of salt.

Strawberry, Fennel, and Arugula Salad

- **Prep:** 15 min
- **Storage:**
  Greens/Fennel/Strawberries/Mint (no **dressing): Fridge 1 day**

This vibrant salad, starring spring strawberries and arugula, helps break boring salad routines while packing anticancer and anti-inflammatory benefits. With mint and lemony vinaigrette, it's a fresh, exciting burst of flavor.

Ingredients

- 4 cups tightly packed baby arugula
- 1 cup thinly sliced fennel
- 12 strawberries, sliced
- 2 tablespoons chopped fresh mint
- 6 tablespoons Lemony Balsamic Vinaigrette
- ¼ cup sliced almonds, toasted

Directions

- In a large bowl, toss together the arugula, fennel, strawberries, and mint. Drizzle with vinaigrette and mix once more. Sprinkle the almonds on top.
- Variations: Substitute toasted walnuts for the almonds. Feel free to sprinkle in some crumbled organic goat cheese.

Walnut, Date, and Herb Salad

- **Prep:** 5 min
- **Storage:** N/A

This salad, born from a finger-food meltdown, tosses dates, arugula, goat cheese, walnuts, and mint into one delicious, vibrant bowl. Dates shine here, offering ancient, longevity-boosting sweetness.

Ingredients

- 4 cups tightly packed baby arugula
- ½ cup loosely packed fresh parsley leaves
- ¼ cup loosely packed fresh mint leaves
- ½ cup walnuts, toasted
- ¼ cup chopped dates
- 4 ounces organic chèvre or other soft goat cheese, crumbled
- ½ cup Lemony Balsamic Vinaigrette

Directions

- Toss the rocket, parsley and mint in a bowl until combined. Add the walnuts, dates, and chèvre, then sprinkle with the vinaigrette and toss again.

Latin Kale

- **Prep: 10 min**
- **Cook: 45 min**
- **Storage: Fridge 4 days**

Toasted cumin, pumpkin seeds, and a splash of lime give this kale dish a vibrant Latin flair. It's fresh, flavorful, and full of zest.

Ingredients

- 8 cups stemmed and chopped lacinato kale, in bite-size pieces
- 2 tablespoons extra-virgin olive oil
- 2½ cups sliced red onions, in half-moons
- Sea salt
- 3 cloves garlic, minced
- ¼ teaspoon cumin seeds, toasted
- Pinch of cayenne
- 1½ teaspoons freshly squeezed lime juice
- 1½ teaspoons freshly squeezed lemon juice
- 1 teaspoon grated lemon zest
- ½ teaspoon Grade B maple syrup
- 2 tablespoons pumpkin seeds, toasted, for garnish

Directions

- Place the kale in a large basin and cover with cold water. Set aside.
- In a big, deep skillet, heat the olive oil on medium-high. Sauté the onions with a touch of salt for 3 minutes. Reduce the heat to medium-low and simmer, stirring periodically, until the onions turn slightly brown, about 5 minutes.
- Turn up the heat to medium. Sauté the garlic, cumin, cayenne, and a pinch of salt for 3 to 4 minutes. Drain the kale, then add it to the skillet and cook until brilliant green and wilted, about 4 minutes. Cover

- and cook for approximately 4 minutes, or until just tender.
- In a small mixing dish, combine the lime juice, lemon juice, lemon zest, and maple syrup. Drizzle over the kale, then remove from the fire and mix until combined. Sprinkle pumpkin seeds over the top.

Sweet-and-Sour Asian Cabbage and Kale

- **Prep: 12 min**
- **Cook: 8 min**
- **Storage: Fridge 4 days**

Tamari, ginger, sesame oil, and lime create a bold, sweet-and-sour flavor that brings an Asian twist to your table. Plus, cabbage stars as a must-have superfood.

Ingredients
- 1 tablespoon plus 2 teaspoons tamari
- 1 tablespoon freshly squeezed lime juice
- 1 tablespoon Grade B maple syrup
- 1 teaspoon toasted sesame oil
- 1 teaspoon grated fresh ginger
- 2 tablespoons extra-virgin olive oil
- 4 cups stemmed and chopped lacinato kale, in bite-size pieces
- Sea salt
- 2 cups shredded red cabbage
- 1 tablespoon sesame seeds, toasted

Directions
- In a small bowl, mix together the tamari, lime juice, maple syrup, toasted sesame oil, and ginger.
- Heat the olive oil in a big, deep skillet over medium-high heat. Sauté the kale with a touch of salt for 4 minutes. Sauté the cabbage with another pinch of salt for 2 minutes. Cook the tamari mixture for about 2 minutes, or until soft. Serve immediately, sprinkled with sesame seeds.

Indian Greens

- **Prep: 10 min**
- **Cook: 8 min**
- **Storage: Fridge 4 days**

This fiber- and protein-packed bowl stars chickpeas, coconut milk, curry, and turmeric for a flavor explosion. It's delicious and loaded with powerful anti-inflammatory benefits.

Ingredients
- 8 cups stemmed and chopped Swiss chard, in bite-size pieces
- 2 tablespoons extra-virgin olive oil
- ¼ teaspoon cumin seeds

- ¼ teaspoon black or brown mustard seeds
- 1 teaspoon grated fresh ginger
- ½ teaspoon turmeric
- ¼ teaspoon curry powder
- ⅛ teaspoon freshly ground black pepper
- Sea salt
- 1 cup canned diced tomatoes, juices reserved
- 1 cup canned chickpeas, drained, rinsed, and mixed with a spritz of lemon
- juice and a pinch of sea salt
- ¼ cup coconut milk
- ¼ teaspoon Grade B maple syrup

Directions
- Cover the chard with cold water in a large bowl and set it away.
- Warm the olive oil in a big, deep pan over medium-high heat. Put in the mustard and cumin seeds and cook them until they start to pop. Add the ginger right away and stir it in. After you add the chard, curry powder, pepper, salt and 2 tablespoons of tomato juice, mix everything together. Put it on for two minutes. The tomatoes and beans should be added and cooked for three minutes. Add the maple syrup and coconut milk, and mix well. Serve right away.
- If you don't have any cumin, mustard seeds, or turmeric on hand, leave them out of the recipe. Add two and a half teaspoons of curry powder to the chard and ginger that you are sautéing.

Mediterranean Greens

- **Prep: 10 min**
- **Cook: 8 min**
- **Storage: Fridge 4 days**

This dish is a Mediterranean adventure, blending Greek olives and feta, Sicilian currants, and Cypriot garlic and mint. Lemon and orange zest add a bright, zesty finish.

Ingredients
- 6 cups stemmed and chopped lacinato kale, in bite-size pieces
- 2 teaspoons freshly squeezed lemon juice
- 1 teaspoon freshly squeezed orange juice
- 2 teaspoons grated lemon zest
- 1 teaspoon grated orange zest
- ½ teaspoon Grade B maple syrup
- ⅛ teaspoon freshly grated nutmeg
- 1 tablespoon currants
- 2 tablespoons extra-virgin olive oil
- 2 cloves garlic, minced
- Pinch of red pepper flakes
- Scant ¼ teaspoon salt
- 1 tablespoon water
- ¼ cup kalamata olives, sliced

- ¼ cup crumbled organic goat's milk or sheep's milk feta cheese
- 2 teaspoons chopped fresh mint, for garnish

Directions
- Cover the kale with cold water in a big bowl and set it aside.
- Lemon juice, orange juice, maple syrup, nutmeg, and lemon zest should all be put in a small bowl and mixed together. Do not beat the currants in.
- Warm up the olive oil in a big, deep pan over medium-low heat. It will take about 20 seconds of cooking after adding the garlic and red pepper flakes for the garlic to turn a light brown colour. Put the kale, salt, and 1 tablespoon of water in the pan. It will take about 4 minutes of cooking until the kale turns bright green and wilts. After you add the olives and currants with their liquid, sauté for about 4 minutes, or until the kale is just barely soft. Take it off the heat, add the feta cheese and mint, and serve right away.

Chapter 6
Protein-Building Foods

Layered Frittata with Leeks, Swiss Chard, and Tomatoes

- **Prep: 10 min**
- **Cook: 25 min**
- **Storage: Fridge 3 days**

Eggs are a healthy, brain-boosting protein, not the cholesterol villains they were once thought to be. In this vibrant frittata, they highlight Swiss chard, cherry tomatoes, and Parmesan in true Italian style.

Ingredients
- 6 organic eggs, beaten
- 2 tablespoons organic plain Greek yogurt
- 2 teaspoons chopped fresh thyme
- ¼ teaspoon freshly ground black pepper
- ⅛ teaspoon freshly grated nutmeg
- Sea salt
- 2 tablespoons extra-virgin olive oil
- 2 cups thinly sliced leeks, white and green parts
- 4 cups stemmed and chopped Swiss chard, in bite-size pieces
- 1 cup cherry tomatoes, halved
- 3 tablespoons almond flour, homemade or store-bought
- 2 tablespoons freshly grated organic Parmesan cheese

Directions
- One rack should go about 6 inches below the grill, and the other should go in the middle of the oven. Warm the oven up to 375°F.
- Place the yoghurt, eggs, thyme, pepper, nutmeg, and ½ teaspoon of salt in a bowl. Add the yoghurt and whisk it until the eggs are foamy and there are only a few small yoghurt lumps left.
- In a pan that can go in the oven, heat the olive oil over medium-low heat. Set the leeks and a pinch of salt on high heat. Cook for about 6 minutes, until they are just golden. Add the Swiss chard on top of the leeks and sprinkle a little salt on top of it. Cover the chard and steam it for

- about two minutes, or until it starts to wilt. Put the tomatoes on top of the chard.
- Spread the egg mix over the tomatoes and make sure it gets through the greens. You might need to gently move the greens around to help this happen. Add the almond flour and Parmesan cheese on top.
- For 10 to 15 minutes, or until the eggs are set, bake on the middle rack of the oven. Move the pan to the top rack and turn the oven on broil. Put the pan under the grill for one minute, or until the almond and cheese flours turn golden brown. You can serve it hot or cold.
- You can make this frittata dairy-free by leaving out the cheese and adding 2 tablespoons of water instead of the yoghurt. You can use spinach or kale instead of the chard if you want to.

Good Mood Sardines

- **Prep: 5 min**
- **Storage: Fridge 3 days**

Sardines, packed with omega-3s and vitamin D, are like little mood boosters in a can. With a little magic—using herbs, olive oil, and lemon—they can turn even skeptics into fans.

Ingredients
- 4 teaspoons freshly squeezed lemon juice
- 2 teaspoons grated lemon zest
- 1 tablespoon finely diced red onion
- 2 teaspoons finely chopped fresh parsley
- 2 teaspoons finely chopped fresh basil
- 2 teaspoons finely chopped fresh mint
- 1 teaspoon extra-virgin olive oil
- 1 teaspoon Dijon mustard
- 1/8 teaspoon sea salt
- 1 (4.35-ounce) can sardines, packed in water or olive oil

Directions
- Rub the red onion, parsley, basil, mint, thyme, olive oil, mustard, and salt together in a bowl. Add the lemon juice and zest. Add the sardines and use a fork to break them up into big chunks. Mix everything together slowly. Add a pinch of salt or a big squeeze of lemon juice based on your taste.

Roasted Halibut with Lime and Papaya and Avocado Salsa

- **Prep:** 5 min
- **Cook:** 12 min
- **Storage:** Fridge 5 days

This bold halibut dish, perfect for tacos or tostadas, is rich in omega-3s with a mild, kid-friendly flavor. A zesty marinade and vibrant papaya-avocado salsa take it over the top.

Ingredients
- 3½ tablespoons freshly squeezed lime juice
- 1 teaspoon grated lime zest
- ¼ teaspoon sea salt
- ¼ teaspoon ground cumin
- Pinch of cayenne
- 1 tablespoon extra-virgin olive oil
- 2 teaspoons finely chopped fresh cilantro
- 4 (6-ounce) halibut fillets
- Papaya and Avocado Salsa

Directions
- Salt, cumin, cayenne, olive oil, cilantro, and lime juice should all be mixed together in a small bowl using a whisk. 3 tablespoons of the marinade should be spread out on both sides of the fillet. Save the rest of the sauce. For 30 minutes, cover and put in the fridge.
- Warm the oven up to 400°F. Lightly oil a pan that can go in the oven that is big enough to fit all of the fillets in one layer.
- Put the pieces in the pan that has been prepared. Use paper towels to dry them off. Bake for 10 to 12 minutes, or until the meat is dark and falls apart easily. To be sure the fish is cooked all the way through, stick a two-pronged cooking fork straight into the meat. The fish is done when it is no longer see-through.
- Pour the marinade you saved over the fish, and then put a lot of salsa on top of each one. Serve right away.
- Variations: Try making soft tacos or tostadas with this recipe. Put a corn tortilla in a warm pan and heat it all the way through for each soft taco. Then, spread 1 tablespoon of Avocado Cream with Basil on one side of the tortilla. Add ¼ cup of Mexican Cabbage Crunch, 2 to 4 ounces of flaked halibut, and 1 tablespoon of Papaya and Avocado Salsa to the tortilla. Fold the tortilla over the ingredients and enjoy. Put corn tortillas in an oven set to 350°F for 15 minutes to make them crisp. Spread the toppings out evenly on top of the tacos.

Black Cod with Miso-Ginger Glaze

- **Prep:** 5 min (+30 min marinating)
- **Cook:** 7 min

- **Storage: Fridge 1 day**

Inspired by my great-grandmother's love for sablefish and Okinawan flavors, this dish blends tradition with a twist. Miso, mirin, ginger, and sesame oil transform black cod into a rich, healthy meal.

Ingredients
- ¼ cup mirin
- 3 tablespoons light miso
- 3 tablespoons freshly squeezed lime juice
- 1½ teaspoons grated fresh ginger
- 1 teaspoon toasted sesame oil
- 4 (4-ounce) black cod fillets, bones removed
- 2 tablespoons chopped fresh cilantro, for garnish
- 1 tablespoon slivered scallion, white and green parts, for garnish

Directions
- Lightly oil a pan that can go in the oven that is big enough to fit all of the fillets in one layer. Add the ginger, lime juice, miso, and sesame oil to a small bowl. Use a whisk to mix the ingredients well. Wash the fillets and dry them with a paper towel. Place the fillets in the pan that has been made. Brush one tablespoon of the miso mixture on each one, making sure it covers both sides. Keep the rest of the mixture for later. For 30 minutes, cover and put in the fridge.
- One rack should go about 4 inches below the grill, and the other should go in the middle of the oven. Warm the oven up to 375°F.
- Place the fillets in the middle of the oven and bake for 5 to 6 minutes, or until the meat looks opaque and starts to flake if they are thick. Move the fillets to the top rack of the oven and turn the oven on broil. Broil for three to four minutes, until the top is brown and browned.
- In the meantime, put the miso mixture you saved aside in a small pot and heat it over medium-low heat until it begins to bubble. Pour the sauce over the fillets, top with the scallions and parsley, and serve right away.
- To increase the ginger flavor, add another teaspoon of freshly grated ginger to the reserved miso mixture while heating in the pot. Ginger has strong enzymes that will break down the fish, making it mealy, so don't add it before soaking the fish.

Roasted Wild Salmon with Olive and Mint Vinaigrette

- **Prep:** 5 min (+20 min marinating)
- **Cook:** 10 min
- **Storage:** Fridge 1 day

Wild salmon, unlike farmed, is rich in heart-healthy omega-3s thanks to its ocean-fed energy stores. This simple, flavorful recipe pairs its natural richness with a fresh mint and olive vinaigrette

Ingredients
- 2 teaspoons extra-virgin olive oil
- 2 teaspoons grated lemon zest
- 2 teaspoons Dijon mustard
- 4 (4-ounce) wild salmon fillets, pinbones removed
- 2 tablespoons water
- ¼ teaspoon sea salt
- Freshly ground black pepper
- ¼ cup Olive and Mint Vinaigrette

Directions
- In a small bowl, mix together the olive oil, lemon zest, and mustard. Place the salmon in an ovenproof baking sheet so that it fits in a single layer without overlap. Distribute the olive oil mixture equally over both sides of the fillet. Cover and place in the refrigerator for 20 minutes.
- Preheat the oven to 400° Fahrenheit.
- Take the salmon out of the refrigerator and add the water.
- Sprinkle the fillets with salt and pepper. Bake for 7 to 9 minutes, or until an instant-read thermometer reads 127°F, depending on the thickness of the fillets; the salmon should be opaque and flaking.
- Whisk the vinaigrette until equally combined, then drizzle over the fillets and serve immediately.
- Variation: Instead of the Olive and Mint Vinaigrette, top the fish with Indonesian Drizzle or Citrus and Mint Yogurt Sauce.

Smoked Salmon Nori Rolls

- **Prep:** 20 min
- **Storage:** Fridge 1 day

This healthy twist on lox and cream cheese uses nutrient-rich nori, smoked wild salmon, and a creamy edamame-wasabi spread. Packed with veggies like avocado, red pepper, and cucumber, it's light, flavorful, and energizing.

Ingredients
- 8 sheets of nori
- 1 cup Edamame Wasabi Spread
- 8 pieces (4 ounces) of smoked wild salmon, spritzed with lime juice
- 1 English cucumber, thinly sliced lengthwise into 16 pieces
- 1 large red bell pepper, thinly sliced lengthwise into 16 pieces

- 2 avocados, thinly sliced lengthwise into 16 pieces
- 24 fresh mint leaves
- 24 fresh cilantro leaves

Directions

- Put a sheet of nori on a work area, rough side up. Spread 2 teaspoons of the edamame wasabi mixture on the nori, leaving 1½ inches bare along the bottom border (facing you) and ½ inch bare along the top. Place one piece of salmon, two slices of cucumber, two slices of bell pepper, and two slices of avocado about 1½ inch from the bottom border. Garnish with three mint leaves and three cilantro leaves. Begin by rolling the nori around the fillings, carefully pressing to create a compact roll. Moisten a finger with warm water and run it along the inside edge of the flap that remains at the top of the roll before pressing it against the roll to seal. Proceed with the remaining ingredients. A sharp serrated knife can be used to cut each roll into eight pieces.
- Variations: To make a vegetarian nori wrap, replace thinly sliced tofu for the salmon. To provide a more exotic flavour, replace the Edamame Wasabi Spread with Indonesian Pesto

Wild, Wild Salmon Burgers

- **Prep: 15 min**
- **Cook: 6 min**
- **Storage: Fridge 5 days**

These wild salmon and wild rice cakes skip the fillers, offering rich omega-3s, B vitamins, fiber, and zinc. Topped with a healthy yogurt sauce, they're a gluten-free, flavor-packed twist on classic fish cakes.

Ingredients

- 1 pound wild salmon fillet, cut into ½-inch chunks
- 1 cup cooked wild rice
- ¼ cup finely chopped scallion, white and green parts
- 1 tablespoon grated lemon zest
- ½ teaspoon sea salt
- ⅛ teaspoon cayenne
- ¼ cup chopped fresh parsley
- 1 tablespoon chopped fresh mint
- 1 tablespoon extra-virgin olive oil
- Yogurt Sauce with Citrus and Mint

Directions

- Place the salmon, wild rice, scallion, lemon zest, salt, and cayenne in a food processor and pulse approximately six times, just until well blended; don't overprocess or you'll end up with a paste.
- Transfer to a mixing bowl, then toss

- in the parsley and mint. Form the mixture into four 4 ounce patties.
- In a large skillet set over medium-high heat, heat the olive oil. When the oil begins to shimmer, add the salmon patties and cook for approximately 3 minutes, or until golden brown on the bottom. Flip them gently and cook for another 3 minutes, or until golden brown on the other side.
- Variation: Replace wild rice with cooked long-grain brown rice, as brown basmati or brown jasmine rice.

Shrimp Via My Ma

- **Prep: 10 min**
- **Cook: 15 min**
- **Storage: Fridge 5 days**

This lemony shrimp dish, inspired by a family recipe, evolved over years into a fresh, protein-packed favorite. With shrimp's rich supply of protein, B12, and omega-3s, it's perfect served over saffron rice and broccoli.

Ingredients

- 3 tablespoons extra-virgin olive oil
- 1 cup diced onion
- ½ cup diced fennel
- ½ cup diced red bell pepper, raw or roasted
- Sea salt
- 2 teaspoons minced garlic
- ¼ teaspoon red pepper flakes
- 1 tablespoon tomato paste
- 1 (14.5-ounce) can diced tomatoes
- 2 teaspoons chopped fresh thyme, or ½ teaspoon dried
- 1 teaspoon chopped fresh oregano, or ¼ teaspoon dried
- 1 pound shrimp, peeled and deveined
- 2 teaspoons freshly squeezed lemon juice
- 2 teaspoons grated lemon zest
- 2 tablespoons finely chopped fresh parsley

Directions

- In a large heavy skillet, heat the olive oil over medium heat. Sauté the onion, fennel, bell pepper, and a generous pinch of salt until the onion is golden, about 8 minutes. Sauté the garlic and red pepper flakes for one minute. Stir in the tomato paste, then add the tomato juice to deglaze the skillet, swirling to dislodge any particles that have adhered to the bottom. Cook until the liquid is reduced by a quarter. Add tomatoes, thyme, oregano, and a pinch of salt. Cook until liquid is reduced by one-quarter. Add the prawns and a touch of salt, stirring gently to mix. Cover and cook for about 3 minutes, or until the shrimp is barely cooked through and opaque. Gently incorporate the

- lemon juice, lemon zest, and parsley. Taste; you may want to add more salt, lemon zest, or a spritz of lemon juice. Serve immediately.

Pan-Seared Scallops with Citrus Drizzle

- **Prep: 10 min**
- **Cook: 5 min**
- **Storage: Fridge 2 days**

Perfectly cooked scallops depend on great timing—keep them between 150°F and 155°F to stay tender, not rubbery. Use an instant-read thermometer and ignore the phone while they sizzle!

Ingredients

- 2 cups tightly packed baby spinach or arugula
- 12 dry-packed sea scallops
- 1 tablespoon extra-virgin olive oil
- 1 tablespoon organic butter or ghee
- 1 teaspoon sea salt
- ½ teaspoon freshly ground black pepper
- 1 tablespoon freshly squeezed orange juice, preferably blood orange juice
- 2 tablespoons freshly squeezed lemon juice, preferably Meyer lemon juice
- 1 tablespoon Many-Herb Gremolata

Directions

- Divide the greens across four plates. Rinse the scallops thoroughly and pat them dry with paper towels. This step is critical, especially if you're using frozen scallops; if they're not dry, you'll boil them instead of searing.
- In a large skillet, warm the olive oil and butter over medium-high heat. Sprinkle the scallops with salt and pepper, and then add them to the pan one at a time in a single, spaced-out layer. If necessary, cook them in two batches. Allow to sear undisturbed for about 2 minutes, or until the bottom is a deep golden brown. Sear scallops on the other side until golden and internal temperature reaches 150°F-155°F. They should be firm to the touch. Remove from the heat and arrange three scallops atop the greens on each plate.
- Place the skillet over medium-low heat and deglaze with the orange juice, lemon juice, and a pinch of salt, stirring to loosen any bits that have stuck to the pan. Cook for about 1 minute, or until the sauce bubbles and thickens slightly. Spoon the mixture over the scallops and top with gremolata.

Greek Chicken Salad

- **Prep:** 15 min
- **Storage:** Fridge 2 days

This refreshing Greek salad combines hydrating cucumbers, tomatoes, parsley, and mint with feta, olives, and capers for a cool, Mediterranean-inspired dish. It's the perfect cure for a hot summer kitchen!

Ingredients
- 1 cup diced cooked organic chicken
- 12 cherry tomatoes, halved
- 1 small cucumber, peeled, seeded, and diced small
- 6 kalamata olives, sliced lengthwise
- 1 tablespoon extra-virgin olive oil
- 2 teaspoons freshly squeezed lemon juice
- 1 teaspoon capers, rinsed and minced
- Pinch of sea salt
- 6 cups loosely packed arugula
- ¼ cup crumbled organic goat's milk or sheep's milk feta cheese
- 1 tablespoon chopped fresh flat-leaf parsley
- 1 tablespoon chopped fresh mint
- Freshly ground black pepper

Directions
- Place the chicken, tomatoes, cucumber, olives, olive oil, lemon juice, capers, and salt in a mixing bowl and mix thoroughly.
- Distribute the rocket across individual plates. Place a mound of chicken salad on top, followed by the feta cheese, parsley, mint, and a few grinds of pepper.
- Variations: Try this as a sandwich filling in whole wheat pita pockets or a Latin-inspired salad with diced avocado, black beans, lime juice, and salt. Remove the feta cheese and substitute 1 tablespoon chopped fresh cilantro for the mint. Toss the chicken with olive and mint vinaigrette or lime vinaigrette with toasted cumin seeds instead of lemon, olive oil, and capers.

Chapter 7
Nibbles and Noshes

Apple Slices with Banana and Almond Butter

- **Prep: 10 min**
- **Storage: N/A**

Crisp apples satisfy sweet cravings while delivering fiber to help balance blood sugar. Topped with almond butter, banana, cinnamon, and dark cocoa, this healthy treat beats any cookie.

Ingredients
- 1 apple, cored and sliced into ½-inch rounds
- 1 tablespoon almond butter
- ½ banana, thinly sliced
- ⅛ teaspoon ground cinnamon
- ¼ teaspoon unsweetened cocoa powder

Directions
- Place the apple slices on a plate and spread almond butter over each one. Place the bananas on top and sprinkle with cinnamon and chocolate powder.
- Optional: Top with unsweetened shredded dried coconut if desired.

Sweet Potato Bars

- **Prep: 15 min**
- **Cook: 40 min (+2 hrs chilling)**
- **Storage: Fridge 4 days / Freezer 2 months**

These sweet potato bars, with a nutty gluten-free crust, are a healthier take on classic lemon bars. Packed with antioxidants and fiber, they're rich, satisfying, and delicious in every bite.

Ingredients

CRUST
- ¾ cup rolled oats
- ¼ cup teff flour or brown rice flour
- ¼ cup shelled unsalted pistachios
- ¼ cup pecans
- ½ teaspoon ground cinnamon
- ½ teaspoon grated orange zest
- ¼ teaspoon sea salt

- 2 tablespoons Grade B maple syrup
- 2 tablespoons extra-virgin olive oil

FILLING

- 1 pound orange-fleshed sweet potatoes, such as garnet yams, baked until tender
- 2 organic eggs, beaten
- ⅓ cup organic plain yogurt
- 3 tablespoons Grade B maple syrup
- ½ teaspoon grated orange zest
- ½ teaspoon ground cardamom
- ½ teaspoon ground ginger
- Freshly grated nutmeg, for dusting

Directions

- Warm the oven up to 375°F before you start making the crust. Coat an 8-inch square baking pan with a little oil.
- Put the oats, teff flour, nuts, pistachios, cinnamon, orange zest, and salt in a food processor. Pulse the ingredients a few times until the mixture looks like coarse cornmeal. Pulse the ingredients together with the maple syrup and olive oil until they are well mixed but still look like crumbles. Put the mixture in the pan that has been prepared and press it hard and evenly into the bottom of the pan. There's no need to clean the blender. Put in the oven for 15 minutes or until it's set. Don't turn off the oven.
- Make the filling at the same time. Put the sweet potato meat in a bowl and mash it up. In a food processor, put 1½ cups of the mashed sweet potatoes. Save any extra for another use. Put in the yoghurt, eggs, maple syrup, orange zest, cardamom, and ginger. Process until the paste is smooth.
- Pour the filling over the base and use a spatula to smooth the top. Then put the bars together and bake them. Add nutmeg on top. It should be baked for about 25 minutes, or until the filling is set and just starting to come away from the pan's sides. Cover, put in the fridge for at least two hours, and then cut into sixteen squares. Let it cool fully on a wire rack.

Wendy's Wunderbars

- **Prep: 25 min**
- **Cook: 1 hr (chilling)**
- **Storage: Fridge 4 days / Freezer 2 months**

Wendy's Wunderbars, packed with dark chocolate, pistachios, almonds, and dates, offer quick, healthy energy without the crash. Perfect for when you need a fast, satisfying boost.

Ingredients

- 2 ounces dark chocolate (60 to 72%

- cacao content), finely chopped
- 1 ounce unsweetened baking chocolate, finely chopped
- ⅓ cup shelled pistachios
- ⅓ cup almonds, toasted
- 8 ounces Medjool dates, halved and pitted
- ½ teaspoon vanilla extract
- ⅛ teaspoon sea salt
- ⅓ cup dried cherries

Directions

- Very little Grease a baking dish that is 8 inches square. Wax paper should be cut into two pieces that are the same width as the pan and long enough to go up the sides and spread over the top of the pan. Put one piece in the pan first, and then the other piece should be put on top of it in the opposite direction.
- Place the bowl with the chopped chocolate over a pot of simmering water. Also, make sure the bowl can handle heat. Stir the chocolate around a lot as you heat it until it melts and is smooth. Take it off the heat.
- To make big pieces, put the nuts and almonds in a food processor and pulse it three or four times. Blend the chocolate, vanilla, salt, and dates together. Process the food in a blender until it starts to stick together, like dough. Add the cherries and pulse a few more times until the cherries are broken up into large pieces that are spread out evenly.
- Place on the pan that has been prepared and use your hands to press it into an even layer. Use a spatula to make the top smooth.
- Place the dish in the fridge for about an hour, or until it is hard. Cover with waxed or parchment paper. Lift the sides of the waxed paper off of the pan and place the food on a cutting board while still on top of the paper. Cut it into 16 pieces using an oiled knife to keep it from sticking. Stack the bars and put them in a container with waxed paper between each layer, or wrap each bar in foil and put it in a container. Store in the refrigerator or freezer. Bring to room temperature before you eat.

Gluten-Free Blueberry Mini Muffins

- **Prep: 5 min**
- **Cook: 15 min**
- **Storage: Fridge 5 days / Freezer 3 months**

These gluten-free mini muffins, made with almond flour, offer a gentle energy boost that's easy on digestion. They're a perfect treat, especially for those sensitive to gluten.

Ingredients

- 2 cups almond flour, homemade or store-bought
- ¼ cup maple sugar
- ½ teaspoon baking soda
- ¼ teaspoon sea salt
- 2 organic eggs, beaten
- 2 tablespoons extra-virgin olive oil
- 2 tablespoons honey
- ½ teaspoon vanilla extract
- ½ teaspoon almond extract
- ½ cup frozen blueberries, preferably wild blueberries

Directions

- Warm the oven up to 375°F. For a 24-cup mini muffin tin, grease each muffin cup well or put two paper liners in each one to make it easy to take out.
- Fill a big bowl with almond flour, maple sugar, baking soda, and salt. Gently mix the ingredients together with your fingers until there are no more lumps.
- Put the eggs in a different bowl. While mixing all the time, slowly add the oil and honey. Mix the almond extract and vanilla extract together with a whisk. Add to the almond flour mix and use a rubber spatula to mix it in. Add the blueberries slowly and carefully. Spread the batter out evenly in the muffin cups that have been prepared. The batter should almost reach the top of each cup.
- The muffin tin should be placed on a baking sheet. Bake for about 15 minutes, or until the tops are golden brown and a toothpick inserted in the middle comes out clean.
- Place a wire rack inside the pan and let it cool down. If you didn't use paper liners, loosen the muffins by running a knife or small offset spatula around the sides.
- If you want a chocolatey boost without the blueberries, leave out the blueberries and move ¼ cup of the batter to a small bowl before spooning it into the muffin pan. Add two teaspoons of unsweetened cocoa powder and mix it in. Then add two tablespoons of chopped dark chocolate. In the bottom of each muffin cup, put a large teaspoon of the chocolate mixture. Then, fill the cups with the rest of the batter. Do what it says and let it cool.

Thyme Onion Muffins

- **Prep: 15 min**
- **Cook: 55 min**
- **Storage: Room temp 4 days / Freezer 2 months**

These savory mini muffins blend teff, spelt, walnuts, thyme, and caramelized onion for a cozy, veggie-packed treat. They're so good, you'll forget they're made with vegetables!

Ingredients
- 4 tablespoons extra-virgin olive oil
- 2 cups finely diced onions
- ¾ teaspoon sea salt
- 2 tablespoons chopped fresh thyme, or 2 teaspoons dried
- 2 teaspoon grated lemon zest
- ⅛ teaspoon freshly ground black pepper
- ¾ cup whole wheat pastry flour
- ⅓ cup teff flour or brown rice flour
- ⅓ cup spelt flour
- 2 teaspoons baking powder
- ½ teaspoon baking soda
- ½ teaspoon sea salt
- 2 organic eggs, beaten
- ⅔ cup organic buttermilk or plain yogurt
- ¼ cup water
- 2 tablespoons extra-virgin olive oil
- 1 tablespoon Grade B maple syrup
- 1 tablespoon Dijon mustard
- ¾ cup finely chopped walnuts

Directions
- Warm the oven up to 400°F. Prepare one 24-cup mini muffin tin by heavily oiling each muffin cup, or line each cup with a paper muffin liner.
- Heat 2 tablespoons of the olive oil in a big skillet over medium heat. Put in the onions and ¼ teaspoon of the salt. Lower the heat to medium-low, and cook, stirring every now and then, for 20 to 25 minutes, or until the onions are very soft and just beginning to turn brown. Take it off the heat and stir in the thyme, lemon zest, and pepper.
- Add the flours, baking powder, baking soda, and the last ¼ teaspoon of salt to a bowl. Use a whisk to mix the ingredients together.
- Set the eggs, buttermilk, water, olive oil, maple syrup, and mustard in a separate bowl. Add the milk and whisk to mix. Add the milk to the flour mixture and stir it in slowly. Before the flour is fully wet, add the onion mixture and walnuts and slowly fold them in. Place an equal amount of batter in each muffin cup; do not overfill them.
- When you stick a toothpick in the middle of a muffin and pull it out clean, the muffins are done. Just bake them for 25 to 30 minutes. For a few minutes, let the muffins cool in the pan. Then, move them to a wire rack and let them cool for another fifteen minutes. You can serve it hot or cold.

Silk Road Spiced Walnuts

- **Prep: 5 min**

- **Cook: 15 min**
- **Storage: Fridge 5 days**

Walnuts' groovy shape helps them hold bold flavors like cumin, coriander, and orange juice. Baked to perfection, they're aromatic, antioxidant-rich, and totally addictive.

Ingredients

- 2 tablespoons freshly squeezed orange juice
- ¼ teaspoon orange zest
- 2 teaspoons extra-virgin olive oil
- 1 teaspoon Grade B maple syrup
- ½ teaspoon ground cumin
- ½ teaspoon ground coriander
- ¼ teaspoon sea salt
- ¼ teaspoon ground ginger
- Pinch of cayenne
- 1 cup walnuts
- ¼ cup unsweetened dried cranberries

Directions

- Warm the oven up to 350°F. Lay parchment paper around the edges of a baking sheet with a lip.
- In a small bowl, mix the orange juice, orange zest, olive oil, maple syrup, cumin, coriander, salt, ginger, and chili pepper with a whisk. Mix in the walnuts and cherries, making sure they are covered all over. Place the mixture on the baking sheet that has been lined out evenly.
- For 10 to 15 minutes, or until the liquid is bubbling and mostly gone, and the walnuts are smelling good and getting a little brown. When it's cool enough to touch, use a metal spoon to break up the mixture.
- Variations: Use raisins instead of cranberries. Use almonds instead of some or all of the walnuts or pistachios instead of some of the walnuts. You could even use a mix of all three nuts. After the mix has cooled, add 1 tablespoon of dark chocolate chips and ¼ cup of dried blueberries to make a powerful vitamin trail mix.

Roasted Olives with Citrus and Herbs

- **Prep: 5 min**
- **Cook: 30 min**
- **Storage: Fridge 5 days**

Roasting olives transforms their briny bite into a rich, sweet flavor. Tossed with garlic, fennel seeds, rosemary, red pepper, and Meyer lemon, they're a unique, irresistible treat.

Ingredients

- 2 cups assorted olives, rinsed
- 1 Meyer lemon, cut into quarters
- 2 tablespoons freshly squeezed

- Meyer lemon juice
- 2 tablespoons extra-virgin olive oil
- 4 cloves garlic, slivered
- 1 teaspoon fennel seeds
- ½ teaspoon dried oregano
- ¼ teaspoon red pepper flakes
- 1 sprig fresh rosemary

Directions
- Warm the oven up to 400°F.
- Place the olives in an 8-inch square non-reactive baking sheet.
- Add the olives to a pan and squeeze the juice of four lemon quarters over them. Then add the lemon quarters, olive oil, garlic, fennel seeds, oregano, red pepper flakes, and rosemary. Mix everything together well.
- Set the oven to 300°F. Serve when still heated.

Artichoke, Basil, and Olive Tapenade

- **Prep: 10 min**
- **Storage: Fridge 2 days**

This bold tapenade, made with olives, artichokes, and basil, wakes up your taste buds and encourages mindful snacking. Great on crackers, toast, or sandwiches, it's flavorful and satisfying.

Ingredients

- ½ cup prepared artichoke hearts, quartered (rinsed and spritzed with lemon juice if canned)
- 20 pitted kalamata olives
- ¾ cup loosely packed fresh basil leaves
- 2 tablespoons extra-virgin olive oil
- 1 tablespoon freshly squeezed lemon juice
- 1 teaspoon grated lemon zest
- 1 clove garlic, minced
- ¼ teaspoon sea salt

Directions
- Using a food processor, pulse the ingredients about 15 times, scraping down the sides of the bowl every once in a while, until the mixture is well mixed but still has some texture.

Minted Guacamole with Pomegranate Seeds

- **Prep: 10 min**
- **Storage: Fridge 3 days**

Inspired by a Southwestern restaurant in a ghost town, this guacamole bursts with flavor and festive color from pomegranate seeds. It's a vibrant twist that looks—and tastes—like Christmas.

Ingredients

- 2 avocados, halved and flesh scooped out
- 2 tablespoons finely diced red onion
- 1 tablespoon finely chopped fresh cilantro
- 1 tablespoon finely chopped fresh mint
- 1 tablespoon freshly squeezed lime juice
- ¼ teaspoon sea salt
- Pinch of cayenne
- 3 tablespoons pomegranate seeds

Directions
- Use a fork to mash the avocado in a bowl until it's mostly smooth. Add the pepper, lime juice, onion, cilantro, mint, and stir until everything is well mixed. Add two tablespoons of the pomegranate seeds and mix them in. Add the last tablespoon of pomegranate seeds as a garnish.

Edamame Wasabi Spread

- **Prep: 5 min**
- **Cook: N/A**
- **Storage: Fridge 2 days**

Wasabi, a sneaky cruciferous veggie, and edamame, fresh soy, come together for a bold, brain-clearing kick. This vibrant combo is as nutritious as it is unforgettable.

Ingredients
- 1 cup fresh or frozen shelled edamame, mixed with a spritz of lime juice and a pinch of salt
- ¼ cup water
- 3 tablespoons extra-virgin olive oil
- 2 tablespoons freshly squeezed lime juice
- 1 tablespoon chopped fresh cilantro or parsley
- 2 teaspoons wasabi powder mixed with 1 teaspoon water, or 2 teaspoons wasabi paste
- ½ teaspoon sea salt

Directions
- Put everything in a food processor and blend it until it's smooth. Once you're done, check the FASS. You might want to add some lime juice or salt.
- If you want to make this dip even spicier, add an extra ¼ teaspoon of wasabi powder.

Chapter 8
Dollops of Yum!

Chive Oil

- **Prep: 5 min**
- **Storage: Fridge 2 weeks**

Chives, ancient cousins of onions and garlic, offer a sweet, fresh flavor and may help detoxify the body. This vibrant chive oil adds a bright, fragrant pop to soups, salads, and fish.

Ingredients
- ½ cup chopped fresh chives
- ½ cup extra-virgin olive oil
- Pinch of sea salt

Directions
- Use a mixer to blend everything together until it's smooth.

Basil Pistachio Pesto

- **Prep: 5 min**
- **Storage: Fridge 5 days / Freezer 2 months**

Pistachios, rich in potassium and B6, bring a buttery, addictive flavor to this fresh twist on classic pesto. It's so irresistible, guests usually start dipping before it even hits the table.

Ingredients
- 1 cup tightly packed fresh basil leaves
- ½ cup shelled raw pistachios
- ⅓ cup extra-virgin olive oil
- 1 tablespoon freshly squeezed lemon juice
- ¼ teaspoon sea salt
- ¼ teaspoon freshly ground black pepper
- 1 tablespoon water (optional)

Directions
- You can use a food processor to mix the basil, pistachios, olive oil, lemon juice, salt, and pepper together. When you add the water, mix the pesto for a short time again. Make sure the FASS is correct. You might want to add some salt or lemon juice.

Ancho Chile Relish

- **Prep: 20 min**

- **Storage: Fridge 5 days**

Ancho chiles bring mild heat and anti-inflammatory benefits to this rich, sultry relish. Blended with garlic, onion, lime, and spices, it's bold without being overpowering.

Ingredients
- 2 dried ancho chiles
- ⅓ cup finely diced red onion
- ⅓ cup chopped fresh cilantro
- 1 teaspoon minced garlic
- 1 teaspoon dried oregano
- ¼ teaspoon ground cumin
- ¼ teaspoon sea salt
- ⅛ teaspoon ground cinnamon
- 2 tablespoons freshly squeezed lime juice
- 1 tablespoon extra-virgin olive oil
- 1¼ teaspoons Grade B maple syrup

Directions
- For about 15 minutes, soak the dried chiles in hot water. (Using a sharp knife, puncture a hole in the chile so that it soaks rather than floats! Remove and throw away the wet liquid. Put the chopped chiles in a small bowl after taking out the seeds. Put in the garlic, oregano, cumin, salt, cinnamon, onion, parsley, olive oil, and maple syrup. Stir everything together. Add a splash of lime juice if you think it needs it.

Many-Herb Gremolata

- **Prep: 5 min**
- **Storage: Fridge 5 days**

Gremolata, a classic Milanese condiment, is simply a mix of chopped herbs, garlic, and lemon zest. It's easy, fresh, and much fancier sounding than it really is.

Ingredients
- ¼ cup finely chopped fresh parsley
- 1 tablespoon finely chopped fresh mint or basil
- 1 tablespoon finely chopped fresh thyme
- Grated zest of 1 lemon
- 1 teaspoon minced garlic

Directions
- Mix the things in a small bowl by stirring them together.

Olive and Mint Vinaigrette

- **Prep: 5 min**
- **Storage: Fridge 5 days**

This lively vinaigrette pairs salty olives with fresh mint for a bold, refreshing zing. Perfect for fish and chicken, it also brings digestive benefits and a boost of vitamin C.

Ingredients
- ¼ cup freshly squeezed lemon juice
- 1 teaspoon Dijon mustard
- ¼ teaspoon sea salt
- ⅛ teaspoon freshly ground black pepper
- 1 tablespoon minced shallot
- ¼ cup extra-virgin olive oil
- ¼ cup kalamata olives, finely chopped
- 2 tablespoons fresh finely chopped fresh mint

Directions
- Salt, pepper, lemon juice, and onion should all be put in a small bowl and mixed together. While whisking, slowly add the olive oil and keep whisking until the mixture is smooth. Put in the mint and olives. Move to a small jar with a lid that fits tightly and give it a good shake.

Indonesian Drizzle

- **Prep: 15 min**
- **Storage: Fridge 2 days**

This Thai-inspired drizzle blends lemongrass with herbs like cilantro, mint, and parsley for a fresh, balanced flavor. It's perfect for adding an Asian accent to fish or chicken dishes.

Ingredients
- ¾ cup loosely packed fresh cilantro leaves
- ¼ cup loosely packed fresh mint leaves
- ¼ cup loosely packed fresh flat-leaf parsley leaves
- 1 tablespoon minced lemongrass
- 2 teaspoons minced fresh ginger
- 1 teaspoon minced garlic
- 3 tablespoons freshly squeezed lime juice
- 3 tablespoons extra-virgin olive oil
- 2 teaspoons fish sauce
- ½ teaspoon Grade B maple syrup
- ⅛ teaspoon sea salt
- Pinch of cayenne

Directions
- Put everything into a blender or food processor and blend or process until the mixture is smooth and creamy. Check the drizzle for sourness. If it tastes too sour, add a pinch of salt.
- Variation: Add ½ cup cashews for delicious pesto.

Lime Vinaigrette with Toasted

Cumin Seeds

- **Prep: 5 min**
- **Storage: Fridge 5 days**

Toasting cumin seeds unlocks rich aroma and powerful health benefits, from aiding digestion to boosting nutrient absorption. This simple vinaigrette captures all that magic in just a few ingredients.

Ingredients

- ¼ cup freshly squeezed lime juice
- 1 teaspoon freshly squeezed lemon juice
- ½ teaspoon grated lemon zest
- ½ teaspoon sea salt
- ⅛ teaspoon cayenne
- 1 teaspoon cumin seeds, toasted
- 1 tablespoon Grade B maple syrup
- ¼ cup extra-virgin olive oil

Directions

- To make the sauce, mix the maple syrup, chili pepper, lemon zest, lime juice, and lemon juice in a small bowl. mixing all the time, slowly add the olive oil and keep mixing until the cream is smooth. Move to a small jar with a lid that fits tightly and give it a good shake.

Lemony Balsamic Vinaigrette

- **Prep: 5 min**
- **Storage: Fridge 1 week (in glass jar)**

This easy, refreshing vinaigrette brightens up all kinds of dishes. It's so simple, you'll want to keep a batch ready at all times.

Ingredients

- 2 tablespoons balsamic vinegar
- 2 tablespoons freshly squeezed lemon juice
- ½ teaspoon grated lemon zest
- ½ teaspoon sea salt
- ½ teaspoon freshly ground black pepper
- ¼ cup extra-virgin olive oil

Directions

- Put the balsamic vinegar, lemon juice, lemon zest, salt, pepper, in a small bowl and stir to mix. mixing all the time, slowly add the olive oil and keep mixing until the cream is smooth. Move to a small jar with a lid that fits tightly and give it a good shake.

Lemon Dijon Vinaigrette

- **Prep:** 5 min
- **Storage:** Fridge 5 days

This lemony vinaigrette adds a fresh, bright lift to anything from salads to marinades. I always keep it on hand for a light, satisfying finish to any meal.

Ingredients
- ¼ cup freshly squeezed lemon juice
- 1 teaspoon Dijon mustard
- ¼ teaspoon sea salt
- ⅛ teaspoon freshly ground black pepper
- 2 tablespoons minced shallot
- ½ teaspoon minced garlic
- ½ cup extra-virgin olive oil

Directions
- In a small bowl, mix together the lemon juice, Dijon mustard, salt, pepper, shallot, and garlic. Slowly add in the olive oil, stirring constantly, until smooth. Move to a small jar with a lid that fits tightly and give it a good shake.

Greener Than Green Goddess Dressing

- **Prep:** 5 min
- **Storage:** Fridge 3 days

This Green Goddess dressing, inspired by my dad, swaps mayo for creamy avocado and yogurt, adding healthy fats and antioxidants. It's vibrant, luscious, and packed with cell-protective power.

Ingredients
- ¾ cup water
- ½ cup organic plain yogurt
- 2 tablespoons freshly squeezed lemon juice
- 2 tablespoons extra-virgin olive oil
- 1 avocado, halved and flesh scooped out
- ¼ cup chopped fresh parsley
- 2 scallions, white and green parts, chopped
- 1 clove garlic, chopped
- ½ teaspoon sea salt

Directions
- Use a blender or food processor to blend or process the food until it is smooth and creamy. Check the FASS. You might want to add a little salt and lemon juice.

Chapter 9
Invigorating Tonics and Elixirs

Chamomile Lemonade with Green Apple

- Prep: 10 min
- Cook: 2 hrs (chilling)
- Storage: Fridge 2 days

This refreshing lemonade blends chamomile tea, green apples, lemon juice, and maple syrup for a calming, summer-ready drink. It's my go-to for easing stress without the heat of a teacup.

Ingredients
- 4 chamomile tea bags
- 4¼ cups boiling water
- 2 green apples, finely grated
- ¾ cup freshly squeezed lemon juice
- 2 teaspoons Grade B maple syrup

Directions
- Place the tea bags in a jar that can handle heat. Add the hot water and let it sit for 4 minutes. Take out the tea bags and add the apples, lemon juice, and maple syrup. Put it away for at least two hours. Clean it with a fine-mesh sieve before you serve it.

Catherine's Survival Shooters

- Prep: 5 min
- Storage: Fridge 1 day

After some trial and error, we cracked the code on a green drink that's both healthy and delicious—thanks to parsley. It delivers a fresh flavor and a powerful antioxidant punch.

Ingredients
- 2 cups chopped pineapple
- 2 cups loosely packed fresh parsley leaves
- 2 cups water
- ¼ cup freshly squeezed orange juice
- 1½ teaspoons grated fresh ginger
- ½ teaspoon freshly squeezed lemon juice

Directions

- When you put the ingredients in a blender, blend them until the mixture is smooth.
- Variations: Instead of pineapple, use mango or papaya. Put a full cup of ice cubes in place of one cup of water to make the drink colder.

Spa in a Pitcher

- **Prep: 5 min**
- **Cook: 1 hr (chilling)**
- **Storage: Fridge 4 days**

Inspired by the classic Pimm's cocktail, this alcohol-free tonic blends citrus, cucumber, mint, and thyme for a spa-like refreshment. It's a beautiful, hydrating drink perfect for hot days.

Ingredients
- 1 orange, thinly sliced into rounds
- 1 Meyer lemon, thinly sliced into rounds
- 1 unpeeled English cucumber, thinly sliced into rounds
- 3 sprigs fresh thyme, tarragon, or mint or fennel fronds, or a combination
- 1 tablespoon freshly squeezed Meyer lemon juice
- 8 cups water or sparkling water

Directions
- Fill a big jug with the lemon, cucumber, herbs, orange, and lemon juice. Using a wooden spoon, press the cucumber, fruit, and herbs against the bottom of the pitcher. Slightly twist and press to release their juices and oils that will evaporate. Put in the water and mix it in. Put it in the fridge for an hour before serving.
- Optional: Instead of water, use 8 cups of hot water and 4 chamomile, ginger, or green tea bags to make a weak tea. Wait until the tea is cool enough to handle before putting it in the pitcher.

Green Tea Cooler with Ginger, Papaya, and Lime

- **Prep: 5 min**
- **Cook: 2 hrs (chilling)**
- **Storage: Fridge 5 days**

Green tea is a powerful immune booster, and papaya brings the sweetness to balance its bitterness. Together, they make a refreshing, longevity-boosting drink with serious health perks.

Ingredients
- 6 green tea bags
- 3 ginger tea bags

- 6 cups boiling water
- 2 cups papaya nectar
- 1 tablespoon freshly squeezed lime juice
- 1 lime, sliced into rounds

Directions

- Put the ginger and green tea bags in a big heat-safe container. Add the boiling water and let the tea steep for 5 minutes. Take out the tea bags and stir in the papaya nectar and lime juice. Add the lime slices and chill in the fridge for at least 2 hours, until very cold.

Simon's Most Nourishing Elixir

- **Prep: 5 min**
- **Cook: 30 min**
- **Storage: Fridge 1 week**

Simon brewed a healing tea for his dad with ginger, cloves, cardamom, citrus zest, and honey—a soothing, flavorful blend straight from the heart. It's love in a cup and a remedy for both body and soul.

Ingredients

- 8 cups water
- 1 (1-inch) piece of ginger
- 1 tablespoon grated Meyer lemon zest
- 2 teaspoons grated tangerine zest
- 1 cinnamon stick
- 5 green cardamom pods
- 4 allspice berries
- 2 whole cloves
- Pinch of saffron
- ¼ cup freshly squeezed Meyer lemon juice
- 2 tablespoons freshly squeezed tangerine juice
- 2 tablespoons honey

Directions

- Spices like cinnamon, allspice, cloves, lemon zest, orange zest, and saffron should all be put in a saucepan with water. The heat should be set to medium-high. Turn down the heat to low, cover, and let it cook for 30 minutes.
- Put the mixture through a fine-mesh sieve into a clean pot. Set the pan on low heat and add the lemon and orange juices. Cook until the food is warm. Add the honey and mix it in. Try it out; you might want to add some honey.

Hibiscus Pomegranate Cooler

- **Prep: 5 min**

- **Cook:** 1 hr (chilling)
- **Storage:** Fridge 4 days

This vibrant drink blends antioxidant-rich pomegranate juice with hibiscus, berries, and orange for a sweet-tart, heart-healthy twist. It's like a Middle Eastern sangria—and maybe a sip of ancient wisdom.

Ingredients

- ¼ cup loose hibiscus tea, or 12 hibiscus tea bags
- 4 cups boiling water
- 4 cups cold water
- 1 cup unsweetened pomegranate juice
- Spritz of fresh lemon juice
- 1 orange, sliced into rounds
- 3 sprigs fresh mint
- 16 frozen strawberries
- 24 frozen blueberries

Directions

- Put the tea in a jar that can handle heat. Add the hot water and let it sit for 5 minutes. Pour the tea through a strainer into a jug. Add the cold water, lemon juice, and pomegranate juice and stir. Then add the mint and orange slices. Put the bowl in the fridge for at least an hour, or until it is very cold. When you are ready to serve, put the frozen blueberries and strawberries in each glass.

Gregg's Morning Protein Shake

- **Prep:** 5 min
- **Storage:** Fridge 2 days (shake or blend before use)

Created for lasting energy and fewer carbs, this high-protein shake blends flaxseeds, rice milk, sunflower seed butter, and berries for great taste and brain-boosting power. It helped lower Gregg's blood pressure and blood sugar—plus, it's quick to make.

Ingredients

- 1½ cups unsweetened plain rice milk or almond milk
- 1½ cups frozen mixed berries, such as blueberries, raspberries, and blackberries
- 1 tablespoon rice protein powder or whey protein powder
- 1 heaping tablespoon sunflower butter or almond butter
- 1 tablespoon ground flaxseeds
- 1 teaspoon honey
- Spritz of fresh lemon juice (optional)

Directions

- Using a blender, blend the flaxseeds, protein powder, milk, berries, and honey until the mixture is smooth. Add a splash of lemon juice if you think it needs it. Serve right away.

Chocolate-Laced Blueberry Cherry Smoothie

- **Prep: 5 min**
- **Storage: Fridge 2 days (shake or blend before serving)**

This rich, chocolate-cherry smoothie is packed with antioxidants, mood-boosting dark chocolate, and anti-inflammatory fruits. With banana, yogurt, and almond butter, it's a decadent-tasting treat that's actually good for you.

Ingredients
- 1 cup organic plain full-fat yogurt
- 1 cup water
- 1 cup frozen banana pieces
- 1 cup frozen cherries
- 1 cup frozen blueberries
- 2 tablespoons unsweetened cocoa powder
- 1 tablespoon almond butter
- ⅛ teaspoon sea salt

Directions
- The banana, cherries, blueberries, cocoa powder, almond butter, and salt should all be put into the blender. Process until smooth. Serve right away.
- Variations: To increase fiber, add 1 tablespoon ground flaxseed. Add a scoop of whey or rice protein powder to get extra protein.

Mango Lassi

- **Prep: 10 min**
- **Storage: Fridge 1 day (shake or blend before serving)**

This refreshing mango lassi blends yogurt with cardamom, a spice that sweetens breath and soothes digestion. Inspired by traditional Indian drinks, it's light, flavorful, and easy to customize with other fruits.

Ingredients
- 2 cups diced fresh or frozen mango
- 1 cup organic plain yogurt
- 1¼ cups plain almond milk
- 1 tablespoon Grade B maple syrup
- Spritz of fresh lemon or lime juice
- ¼ teaspoon ground cardamom
- Pinch of sea salt
- 4 sprigs fresh mint, for garnish

Directions
- In a blender, blend the mango, yogurt, almond milk, maple syrup, lemon juice, cardamom, and salt until the mixture is smooth. Stir in

- the mint and add a splash of lemon or lime juice if you think it needs it. Pour the smoothie into cups and decorate with the mint.

Chapter 10
Sweet Bites

Chocolate-Dipped Cherry Haystacks and Chocolate-Dipped Apricots

- **Prep: 10 min**
- **Cook: 10 min**
- **Storage: Fridge 3 days (bring to room temp before serving)**

These easy chocolate haystacks are perfect for entertaining, with slivered almonds giving them their signature look. Skip the complex tempering—just melt carefully with a touch of oil, and dip quickly for stunning results.

Ingredients
- ½ cup dried cherries or blueberries
- ⅓ cup slivered almonds, toasted
- 2 tablespoons cacao nibs
- 5 ounces dark chocolate (70 to 72% cacao content), finely and uniformly chopped
- 1 teaspoon neutral oil, such as almond or grapeseed oil
- 16 dried apricots
- ½ cup chopped pistachios

Directions
- Put parchment paper on the bottom of a baking sheet. Add the cocoa nibs, cherries, and almonds to a bowl and mix them together.
- A quarter cup of the chopped chocolate should be set away. The rest should be put in a small stainless steel bowl. Put the oil in. In a skillet, bring about an inch of water to a boil. Take it off the heat and place it on a kitchen towel or hot pad on the table. Carefully put the bowl of chocolate into the hot water so that no water gets into the chocolate. Use a spoon to stir the chocolate slowly and continuously until it melts. Take the bowl out of the hot water and add the chocolate that you saved. Stir the chocolate in until it melts. If some chocolate doesn't melt, put the bowl back in the hot water for a few seconds and stir it until it's all smooth and shiny.
- Place the apricots on the baking

- sheet that has been set up. Dip each one in half into the chocolate and then put it on the sheet. Before the chocolate sets, sprinkle the nuts on top.
- Add the last bit of chocolate to the bowl with the cherry mixture. Thoroughly mix everything together. Using a teaspoon, make 16 little haystacks out of the dough on the baking sheet that has been lined with parchment paper. To set the chocolate, put the baking sheet in the fridge for 5 to 10 minutes. You can eat it now or save it for later.

Roasted Strawberries with Pomegranate Molasses and Basil

- **Prep: 10 min**
- **Cook: 1 hr 30 min**
- **Storage: Fridge 4 days / Freezer 3 months**

Slow-roasting strawberries in pomegranate molasses and maple syrup intensifies their flavor into something truly magical. Finished with fresh basil, they're a rich, anti-inflammatory treat perfect for topping desserts.

- 3 tablespoons Grade B maple syrup
- 1 tablespoon pomegranate molasses, homemade or store-bought
- 1½ teaspoons extra-virgin olive oil
- ¼ teaspoon sea salt
- Freshly ground black pepper
- 2 cups strawberries, hulled
- 2 teaspoons very thinly sliced fresh basil

Directions
- Warm the oven up to 250°F. Lay parchment paper around the edges of a baking sheet with a lip.
- Salt, olive oil, a few grinds of pepper, and maple syrup should all be put in a big bowl and mixed together with a whisk. When you add the strawberries, stir them in slowly until they are well covered.
- Spread the strawberry mix out in a single layer on the baking sheet that has been lined with foil. (Save any juices that are left over to put on top of the strawberries or slurp up!) Bake for about 90 minutes, or until the strawberries are about half the size they were at the beginning. Halfway through the baking time, stir and re-arrange the strawberries. After 5 minutes, move the berries and any juices that are still on the pan to a bowl. After adding the basil, stir it in slowly and let it sit for 5 minutes so the tastes can mix. You can serve it hot or cold.

Raspberry Hibiscus Sorbet

- **Prep: 20 min**
- **Cook: 2+ hrs (chilling) + churning/freezing**
- **Storage: Freezer 3 months (cover with plastic wrap or wax paper)**

Inspired by my local sorbet shop, this raspberry-hibiscus-coconut sorbet is rich in flavor and antioxidants—raspberries pack 50% more than strawberries. Just chill, churn, and enjoy a refreshing, nutrient-packed treat.

Ingredients
- 2 hibiscus tea bags
- ½ cup boiling water
- ¾ cup water
- ¼ cup honey
- 1 (12-ounce) package frozen raspberries, or 2 cups fresh raspberries
- ½ cup coconut milk
- ⅛ teaspoon freshly squeezed lime juice

Directions
- Put the tea bags in a small cup or jar that can handle heat. Add the hot water and let it sit for 5 minutes. Take the tea bags out.
- Add the honey and water to a pot and heat it over medium-high. Simmer for a while. After you add the raspberries, stir them in all the time for two to three minutes, or until they start to break apart. Take it off the heat and add the coconut milk and hibiscus tea while whisking. Wait about 10 minutes and then cool down.
- Put it in a blender, add the lime juice, and mix it until it's smooth. Press the mush with the back of a spoon to get as much liquid out as you can through a fine-mesh sieve. Put it in a jar for storage, cover it, and put it in the fridge for at least two hours.
- Take the bowl out of the freezer that makes ice cream. Pour the sorbet mix into the ice cream maker's bowl and mix it with a whisk until it's smooth. Follow the directions given by the maker.
- Move to a container that won't let air in. To keep it from getting freezer burn, put waxed paper or plastic wrap right on top of it, then put the lid on top of it. Once you want it firm, freeze it.

Coffee-Infused Chocolate Sorbet

- **Prep: 20 min**
- **Cook: 4+ hrs (chilling) + churning/freezing**

- **Storage: Freezer 1 month (cover with plastic wrap or wax paper)**

This rich sorbet blends two types of dark chocolate with almond milk and coffee for a feel-good treat that may boost mood, memory, and even health. Just chill, churn, and enjoy dessert with benefits.

Ingredients
- ¼ cup whole coffee beans
- ¾ cup water
- ½ cup Grade B maple syrup
- Pinch of sea salt
- 5 ounces dark chocolate (64 to 70% cacao content), finely chopped
- ⅓ cup unsweetened cocoa powder
- ½ teaspoon vanilla extract
- 1 cup plain almond milk

Directions
- Put the coffee beans in a small plastic bag that can be closed again, and use a rolling pin to break them up into small pieces.
- Stir the water, maple syrup, and salt together in a pot over high heat. Bring to a boil, then turn down the heat to low and let it cook for one minute. Put the coffee beans in, cover, and take the pot off the heat. Give the coffee five minutes to steep.
- Put the chocolate in a bowl that can handle heat. Put a piece of cheesecloth over the bowl and line a sieve with it.
- Bring the coffee infusion back to a simmer over medium heat, then pour it straight through the lined sieve into the chocolate. Let it sit for one minute, and then mix it with a whisk until it's smooth. Whisk in the cocoa powder until it is well mixed and smooth. Then add the vanilla and whisk again.
- Put the mix into a blender, add the almond milk, and blend until it's smooth and foamy. Put the mixed ingredients back into the bowl, cover with plastic wrap, and put it in the fridge for at least 4 hours.
- Take the bowl out of the freezer that makes ice cream. Pour the sorbet mix into the ice cream maker bowl and mix it with a whisk until it is smooth. Follow the directions given by the maker.
- Move to a container that won't let air in. Cover it with plastic wrap right on top to keep it from getting freezer burn. Once you want it firm, freeze it.

Apple-Raspberry Nut Crumble

- **Prep: 10 min**
- **Cook: 45 min**
- **Storage: Fridge 3 days**

This apple crumble with raspberry sauce was born from a happy kitchen accident and blends sweet, tart, and crunchy to perfection. With raspberries, walnuts, and apples, it's a delicious, antioxidant-rich dessert.

Ingredients

FILLING
- 2 teaspoons extra-virgin olive oil
- 3 cups Granny Smith apples, peeled and sliced into ¼-inch-thick wedges
- Pinch of sea salt
- ¼ teaspoon ground cinnamon
- ⅛ teaspoon ground allspice
- Pinch of freshly grated nutmeg
- 1 cup unfiltered apple cider
- 1 cup fresh or frozen raspberries
- ½ teaspoon vanilla extract

TOPPING
- ½ cup coarsely chopped walnuts
- ¼ cup almond flour, homemade or store-bought
- ¼ teaspoon ground cinnamon
- 3 tablespoons Grade B maple syrup
- 1 tablespoon extra-virgin olive oil

Directions
- Warm the oven up to 375°F.
- Warm up the olive oil in a pan over medium-low heat to make the filling. "You can bake the crumble right in the skillet if you use an 8-inch oven-safe skillet." Put in the apple slices and salt. Cook for two minutes. Put in the nutmeg, cloves, and cinnamon. Cook for 3 to 4 minutes, stirring slowly and often. Bring to a boil after adding the apple cider. Turn down the heat and let it cook for about 5 minutes, or until the apples are soft. After taking it off the heat, add the vanilla and cherries and mix them in. Put it in a pie plate. (If you are using an oven-safe pan, you can skip this step.)
- Make the filling at the same time. Add the cinnamon, almond flour, and walnuts to a small bowl and mix them together. Mix the olive oil and maple syrup together in a different small bowl. Add the milk to the walnut paste and mix it well.
- Spread the topping out evenly over the filling to put the crumble together and bake it. Bake for approximately 35 minutes, until the topping is brown and the filling is bubbling. Allow to cool for at least ten minutes. Serve either warm or at room temperature.

Spiced Almond Macaroon Buttons

- **Prep: 15 min**
- **Cook: 15 min**
- **Storage: Room temp 2 days / Freezer 1 month (layered with parchment)**

These light, French-inspired macaroons skip the heavy coconut and refined sugar, using almonds, turbinado, and warm spices like cinnamon and allspice. They're flavorful, satisfying, and even help with bloating—no guilt required.

Ingredients

- 1 cup almond flour, homemade or store-bought
- 3 tablespoons turbinado sugar
- ¼ teaspoon ground cinnamon
- ⅛ teaspoon ground allspice
- Pinch of ground cardamom
- ⅛ teaspoon sea salt
- ¼ cup organic egg whites (about 2 large eggs)
- ¾ teaspoon almond extract
- ¼ teaspoon vanilla extract
- 20 whole almonds, or 1 cup slivered almonds, for decoration

Directions

- Preheat your oven to 350°F. Prepare a baking sheet by lining it with parchment paper.
- Place the almond flour, sugar, cinnamon, allspice, cardamom, and salt in a mixing bowl and blend.
- Place the egg whites in a small basin and lightly whip with a fork to make them easier to measure and pour. Stir in 3 tablespoons of egg whites, almond essence, and vanilla with a spatula. The texture should be wet and squishy, but firm enough to roll into a ball between wet hands. If the dough is too stiff, add little additional egg white.
- Roll a small amount of dough into balls using damp hands. Place them on a baking sheet, about 2 inches apart, and flatten them with a wet finger. Place an almond or a few slivered almonds on top of each cookie. Put them in the oven for 15 minutes, or until the tops are dry and a light golden brown color. Look at the bottoms: they should be golden brown. Transfer to a wire rack and cool completely before serving.

Insanely Good Chocolate Brownies

- **Prep: 20 min**
- **Cook: 30 min**
- **Storage: Fridge 5 days / Freezer 3 months**

These "healthy brownies" swap out white sugar, flour, and butter for maple syrup, almond and brown rice flour, and olive oil—without losing any of the decadence. Packed with dark chocolate, walnuts, and cinnamon, they wowed even the brownie purists.

Ingredients

- ⅓ cup almond flour, homemade or store-bought
- ⅓ cup brown rice flour
- 2 tablespoons natural unsweetened cocoa powder
- ½ teaspoon ground cinnamon
- ½ teaspoon baking soda
- ⅛ teaspoon sea salt
- 8 ounces dark chocolate (68 to 72% cacao content), chopped
- ⅓ cup extra-virgin olive oil
- 2 organic eggs
- ⅓ cup Grade B maple syrup
- ⅓ cup maple sugar
- 1 teaspoon vanilla extract
- ½ cup coarsely chopped walnuts (optional), toasted

Directions

- Preheat the oven to 350° Fahrenheit. Line an 8-inch square baking pan with two layers of foil that are long enough to overlap on all four edges. Lightly grease the foil.
- Combine the almond flour, brown rice flour, cocoa powder, cinnamon, baking soda, and salt in a bowl and whisk until combined.
- Place half of the chocolate in a heatproof bowl and set it over a saucepan of simmering water. Heat, stirring frequently, until the chocolate has melted and smoothed. Remove from the fire and add the olive oil.
- Whisk the eggs in a large bowl until foamy. Whisk in the maple syrup and maple sugar gradually, then continue whisking until the mixture is smooth. Add the vanilla essence, then gradually add the chocolate while beating rapidly, until smooth and shiny.
- Beat in the flour mixture for approximately 1 minute. Add in the remaining chocolate and walnuts. Spread the batter out evenly on top of the pan that has been prepared.
- Bake for 30 minutes, or until a toothpick inserted into the center comes out clean. Allow it cool to room temperature in the pan, then cover and chill for at least an hour before cutting into 16 brownies.
- To make fudgier brownies, add ⅓ cup almond flour instead of rice flour.

Raspberry Pomegranate Sauce

- **Prep: N/A**
- **Cook: 15 min**
- **Storage: Fridge 1 week / Freezer 2 months**

This rich, dreamy sauce blends raspberries and pomegranate molasses into a bold, tangy-sweet drizzle. It's simple, versatile, and healthy enough to pour over dessert without guilt.

Ingredients

- 1 (12-ounce) bag frozen raspberries, or 2 cups fresh raspberries
- 2 tablespoons Grade B maple syrup
- 2 teaspoons pomegranate molasses, homemade or store-bought
- Pinch of sea salt
- 2 tablespoons freshly squeezed orange juice

Directions

- Salt, maple syrup, pomegranate molasses, and raspberries should all be put in a small, heavy pot and mixed together. Bring to a boil while turning often over medium-high heat. Turn down the heat to low and let it cook for one to two minutes, or until most of the berries have broken up. Take it off the heat and wait ten minutes.
- Put it in a blender, add the orange juice, and mix it until it's smooth. Press the mush with the back of a spoon to get as much liquid out as you can through a fine-mesh sieve. Check the FASS; you might need to add more maple syrup.

Yogurt-Berry Brûlée with Maple Almond Brittle

- **Prep: 10 min**
- **Cook: 12 min**
- **Storage: Fridge 5 days / Freezer 1 month**

This crème brûlée-inspired treat swaps custard for sweetened Greek yogurt and skips the torch with an easy oven-baked brittle. Creamy, crunchy, and loaded with health benefits, it's a lighter twist on a classic.

Ingredients

BRITTLE

- 1 teaspoon extra-virgin olive oil
- 3 tablespoons Grade B maple syrup
- 2 tablespoons sliced almonds
- 1/8 teaspoon ground cardamom

MAPLE-SCENTED YOGURT

- 2 cups organic plain Greek yogurt
- 1¼ cups fresh berries, any type
- 1 teaspoon Grade B maple syrup

Directions

- Turn on the oven light and heat the oven to 375°F. This will help you make the brittle. Cover a baking sheet with a rim with parchment paper.
- Using a paper towel or brush, spread the oil out on the parchment paper so that it has a thin, even layer of oil covered it.
- In a small bowl, mix the nuts,

- cardamom, and maple syrup. Put the mixture on the parchment paper that has been greased, and then tilt the pan to make it spread out evenly. Keep the food close to the oven for 5 to 7 minutes. First, the syrup will start to bubble. After another two or three minutes, the almonds will turn a nice golden color, and the syrup will turn a deep brown color. After this, take the brittle out of the oven and let it cool for a while. You can put it in the freezer for five minutes to make it easier to break up. Lift the firm brittle with a thin metal spatula and break it into pieces of different sizes. Use right away or store in a jar that won't let air in.
- To make the yogurt mixture and put the dish together, mix the yogurt, maple syrup, and 1 cup of the berries together slowly in a bowl.
- Place the yogurt mixture on dessert plates, then top with the brittle and the last ½ cup of berries. Do this right before serving.
- Variation: Add Roasted Strawberries and Juices as a layer.

Almond Flour

- **Prep: 10 min**
- **Storage: Fridge 1 week / Freezer 6 months**

Almond flour is a tasty, gluten-free alternative to white flour that's easier to digest and helps regulate blood sugar. It's healthy, versatile, and surprisingly easy to make at home.

Ingredients
- 1 cup raw almonds

Directions
- Put ½ cup of the almonds in a food processor and pulse it a few times to make big chunks. Then pulse until a meal that is medium-fine forms and just starts to stick to the bowl's sides. Watch out not to process too much or you'll get almond butter. Move to a bowl or storage container and do it again with the last ½ cup of almonds. Keep the almond flour in the fridge or freezer in a sealed container if you're not going to use it right away. This will keep it fresh and keep the delicate nut oils from going bad.

Week 1 Shopping List

🌿 Vegetables & Herbs
- Eggplants (2–3 medium)
- Mushrooms (portobello, cremini, or button – 3–4 cups)
- Carrots (with tops, 4–5 large)
- Pumpkin (fresh or canned, ~3–4 cups)
- Chestnuts (roasted or fresh, ~2 cups)
- Purple potatoes (3–4 medium)
- Broccoli stems (from 2–3 heads of broccoli)
- Garlic (1 bulb)
- Fresh oregano (1 bunch)
- Fresh basil (1 bunch)
- Fresh parsley (1 bunch)
- Mixed greens or salad greens (optional, for salad base)

● Pantry Staples & Oils
- Extra virgin olive oil
- Sea salt or kosher salt
- Black pepper
- Apple cider vinegar or white wine vinegar
- Honey or maple syrup (small amount for vinaigrette or soup sweetening)
- Vegetable broth or stock (for soups – ~6–8 cups total)
- Raw cacao powder (for hot chocolate)
- Dark chocolate (70% or more, ~½ cup chips or chopped)
- Walnuts or pine nuts (for pesto – ~½ cup)
- Nutritional yeast (optional, for pesto flavor)
- Pasta (trofie or substitute like fusilli, ~1 package)

🥛 Dairy / Alternatives
- Plant-based milk (almond, oat, or soy – ~2 cups for hot chocolate)
- Optional: Parmesan cheese (if not vegan, for pesto – ~½ cup grated)

🍊 Fruits & Flavorings
- Oranges (2–3 for juice/zest)
- Fresh ginger root (1–2 inches)

Week 1 Meal Plan

Days	Breakfast	Lunch	Dinner
Day 1	Grilled Eggplant	Roasted Mushrooms	Classic Lemon Vinaigrette
Day 2	Ginger Orange Hot Chocolate	Classic Lemon Vinaigrette	Dark Chocolate Breakfast Bar
Day 3	Dark Chocolate Breakfast Bar	Pumpkin Soup	Chestnut Soup
Day 4	Pumpkin Soup	Roasted Purple Potato Soup	Roasted Mushrooms
Day 5	Warm Carrot Top Salad	Pumpkin Soup	Grilled Eggplant
Day 6	Roasted Purple Potato Soup	Chestnut Soup	Broccoli Stem and Oregano Soup
Day 7	Mushroom Soup	Broccoli Stem and Oregano Soup	Basic Pesto with Trofie

Week 2 Shopping List

Vegetables & Herbs
- Eggplants (2–3 medium)
- Mushrooms (portobello, cremini, or button – 4–5 cups)
- Pumpkin (fresh or canned, ~4–5 cups)
- Chestnuts (roasted or fresh, ~2–3 cups)
- Purple potatoes (3–4 medium)
- Broccoli stems (from 2–3 heads of broccoli)
- Carrots (with tops, 3–4 large)
- Garlic (1 bulb)
- Fresh oregano (1 bunch)
- Fresh basil (1 bunch)
- Fresh parsley (1 bunch)
- Mixed greens or salad greens (optional, for salad base)

Pantry Staples & Oils
- Extra virgin olive oil
- Sea salt or kosher salt
- Black pepper
- Apple cider vinegar or white wine vinegar
- Honey or maple syrup (small amount)
- Vegetable broth or stock (for soups – ~6–8 cups total)
- Raw cacao powder (for hot chocolate)
- Dark chocolate (70% or more – ~½ cup chips or chopped)
- Walnuts or pine nuts (for pesto – ~½ cup)
- Nutritional yeast (optional, for pesto)
- Pasta (trofie or similar – ~1 package)

Dairy / Alternatives
- Plant-based milk (almond, oat, or soy – ~2 cups)
- Optional: Parmesan cheese (if not vegan – ~½ cup grated)

Fruits & Flavorings
- Oranges (2–3 for juice/zest)
- Fresh ginger root (1–2 inches)

Week 2 Meal Plan

Days	Breakfast	Lunch	Dinner
Day 1	Basic Pesto with Trofie	Pumpkin Soup	Roasted Mushrooms
Day 2	Mushroom Soup	Dark Chocolate Breakfast Bar	Grilled Eggplant
Day 3	Ginger Orange Hot Chocolate	Chestnut Soup	Roasted Purple Potato Soup
Day 4	Roasted Mushrooms	Warm Carrot Top Salad	Pumpkin Soup
Day 5	Grilled Eggplant	Broccoli Stem and Oregano Soup	Chestnut Soup
Day 6	Pumpkin Soup	Basic Pesto with Trofie	Classic Lemon Vinaigrette
Day 7	Dark Chocolate Breakfast Bar	Ginger Orange Hot Chocolate	Mushroom Soup

Week 3 Shopping List

🌿 Vegetables & Herbs
- Eggplants (2–3 medium)
- Mushrooms (portobello, cremini, or button – 4–5 cups)
- Pumpkin (fresh or canned – ~4 cups)
- Purple potatoes (3–4 medium)
- Carrots (with tops – 3–4 large)
- Chestnuts (roasted or fresh – ~2–3 cups)
- Broccoli stems (from 2–3 heads of broccoli)
- Garlic (1 bulb)
- Fresh basil (1 bunch)
- Fresh oregano (1 bunch)
- Fresh parsley (1 bunch)
- Salad greens or mixed greens (optional for vinaigrette and salad)

● Pantry Staples & Oils
- Extra virgin olive oil
- Apple cider vinegar or white wine vinegar
- Sea salt or kosher salt
- Black pepper
- Honey or maple syrup (small amount, optional)
- Vegetable broth or stock (for soups – ~6–8 cups total)
- Raw cacao powder (for hot chocolate)
- Dark chocolate (70% or higher – ~½ cup chips or chopped
- Walnuts or pine nuts (for pesto – ~½ cup)
- Nutritional yeast (optional, for pesto)
- Pasta (trofie or similar – ~1 package)

🥛 Dairy / Alternatives
- Plant-based milk (almond, oat, or soy – ~2 cups for hot chocolate)
- Optional: Parmesan cheese (if not vegan – ~½ cup grated)

● Fruits & Flavorings
- Oranges (2–3 for juice/zest)
- Fresh ginger root (1–2 inches)

Week 3 Meal Plan

Days	Breakfast	Lunch	Dinner
Day 1	Classic Lemon Vinaigrette	Pumpkin Soup	Roasted Purple Potato Soup
Day 2	Warm Carrot Top Salad	Roasted Mushrooms	Chestnut Soup
Day 3	Grilled Eggplant	Mushroom Soup	Broccoli Stem and Oregano Soup
Day 4	Broccoli Stem and Oregano Soup	Ginger Orange Hot Chocolate	Grilled Eggplant
Day 5	Basic Pesto with Trofie	Warm Carrot Top Salad	Dark Chocolate Breakfast Bar
Day 6	Chestnut Soup	Roasted Purple Potato Soup	Classic Lemon Vinaigrette
Day 7	Pumpkin Soup	Dark Chocolate Breakfast Bar	Mushroom Soup

Week 4 Shopping List

🌿 Vegetables & Herbs
- Eggplants (2–3 medium)
- Mushrooms (portobello, cremini, or button – 4–5 cups)
- Pumpkin (fresh or canned – ~4–5 cups)
- Chestnuts (roasted or fresh – ~2–3 cups)
- Purple potatoes (3–4 medium)
- Carrots (with tops – 3–4 large)
- Broccoli stems (from 2–3 heads of broccoli)
- Garlic (1 bulb)
- Fresh basil (1 bunch)
- Fresh oregano (1 bunch)
- Fresh parsley (1 bunch)
- Mixed greens or salad greens (optional, for vinaigrette or salad)

● Pantry Staples & Oils
- Extra virgin olive oil
- Apple cider vinegar or white wine vinegar
- Sea salt or kosher salt
- Black pepper
- Honey or maple syrup (optional sweetener)
- Vegetable broth or stock (for soups – ~6–8 cups total)
- Raw cacao powder (for hot chocolate)
- Dark chocolate (70% or higher – ~½ cup chips or chopped)
- Walnuts or pine nuts (for pesto – ~½ cup)
- Nutritional yeast (optional, for pesto)
- Pasta (trofie or similar – ~1 package)

🥛 Dairy / Alternatives
- Plant-based milk (almond, oat, or soy – ~2 cups for hot chocolate)
- Optional: Parmesan cheese (if not vegan ~½ cup grated)

● Fruits & Flavorings
- Oranges (2–3 for juice/zest)
- Fresh ginger root (1–2 inches)

Week 4 Meal Plan

Days	Breakfast	Lunch	Dinner
Day 1	Ginger Orange Hot Chocolate	Chestnut Soup	Pumpkin Soup
Day 2	Roasted Purple Potato Soup	Grilled Eggplant	Roasted Mushrooms
Day 3	Warm Carrot Top Salad	Broccoli Stem and Oregano Soup	Mushroom Soup
Day 4	Classic Lemon Vinaigrette	Basic Pesto with Trofie	Chestnut Soup
Day 5	Mushroom Soup	Pumpkin Soup	Roasted Purple Potato Soup
Day 6	Dark Chocolate Breakfast Bar	Ginger Orange Hot Chocolate	Warm Carrot Top Salad
Day 7	Broccoli Stem and Oregano Soup	Classic Lemon Vinaigrette	Basic Pesto with Trofie

Conclusion

Thank you for taking this journey through "The Dr. Li's Diet Cookbook."

Throughout this book, you've learned how the right foods can support your health, strengthen your body, and help you feel more energized and alive. These recipes are not just meals—they are tools for building a better life, inspired by Dr. William W. Li's approach to using food as medicine.

We've focused on simple, wholesome ingredients that anyone can cook with. Whether it's leafy greens, antioxidant-rich berries, or healing spices, each recipe brings something valuable to your table. The more you include these foods in your routine, the more you'll feel the difference in your body and mind.

As you move forward, keep it simple. Choose real food, cook often, and listen to your body. You don't have to be perfect—just be consistent. Your health journey doesn't end here, it begins with every meal you make.

Share your meals with loved ones. Pass on what you've learned. And above all, keep going.

Eat well. Live well. Stay strong. You've got this.

Made in the USA
Monee, IL
15 July 2025

21178685R00057